Mom Loves You Best

Mom Loves You Best
Forgiving and Forging Sibling Relationships

by Cathy Jo Cress, MSW,
and Kali Cress Peterson, MS, MPA

New Horizon Press
Far Hills, NJ

Cress, Cathy Jo and Kali Cress Peterson
Mom Loves You Best: Forgiving and Forging Sibling Relationships

Cover design: Wendy Bass
Interior design: Susan Sanderson

Library of Congress Control Number: 2010925081

ISBN 13: 978-0-88282-321-8
New Horizon Press

Manufactured in the U.S.A.

2014 2013 2012 2011 2010 / 5 4 3 2 1

This book is dedicated to our siblings Harry Steven Cress, Staci Nestaval, Jill Gallo and Scott Peterson and to Dan Murphy, who inspired his wife to live in the here and now.

Authors' Note

This book is based on the authors' research, personal experiences and clients' real life experiences. In order to protect privacy, names have been changed and identifying characteristics have been altered except for contributing experts. For purposes of simplifying usage, the pronouns his/her and s/he are sometimes used interchangeably. The information contained herein is not meant to be a substitute for professional evaluation and therapy with mental health professionals.

Table of Contents

❧ Foreword ❧

Mom Loves You Best is an excellent book that will help siblings learn how to forgive. This is an essential guide to assist wounded brothers and sisters develop compassion for themselves and their siblings as they navigate the aging and death of their parents. The healing power of absolution is highlighted for adult children long estranged by childhood wounds to learn to heal themselves and reconnect with each other. This is no trivial need or accomplishment. So many people come into my forgiveness trainings with unresolved childhood and adolescent issues that flare up as they move through the life cycle. It is clear to me that wounded siblings who read *Mom Loves You Best* will be able to start the process of caring for themselves and find how they can repair long ago childhood damage. This book skillfully teaches siblings to take responsibility for what they feel in the here and now and to learn to communicate with each other from a healthier place. The methodology in *Mom Loves You Best* will help move troubled people to personal peace and can be used as a template for solution, not a rehashing of personal and family strife.

Siblings, like all the people I have worked with at The Stanford Forgiveness Project, need to move from feeling like victims to healthy and happy individuals who can make peace with themselves and their long estranged family members. And let me tell you it is not easy, as little in our culture addresses this yawning need. I have listened to countless people engage in useless arguments with their brothers and sisters over estates, how to care for ill parents, attention to past wounds, selling the family home, etc. Now there is a book that addresses these issues directly.

My work for years has been to encourage people to make peace with their pasts and move on. *Mom Loves You Best* is a companion to my own bestselling book *Forgive for Good* (Harper-One). As a fellow researcher and teacher in forgiveness, I know this book will be a welcome and needed addition to the growing library of forgiveness training and help. And when practiced, the information in this book will reduce suffering in this world.

Dr. Fred Luskin
Author/Co-Founder,
Standford University
Forgiveness Project

How Stories Arise from Generations

Prior generations define your family's rules, from holiday rituals and rites of passage to how parents and children act. A generational group is a set of individuals having common cultural and societal characteristics and attitudes. Essentially, a set of laws, very often unstated, are passed on from great-grandparent to grandparent to parent to child. These play an important role in setting standards for parents to engage with their children and siblings to interact with one another. For example, these laws may dictate a gender bias (e.g. only boys should be given access to higher education). This family precedent is then passed on to each successive generation. At some point these family laws or—in this example—a gender bias, create feelings of ill will between siblings and may play an important part in understanding the origins of your "I Hate You" story.

Finding out the environmental or economic conditions that were present in each cohort tell us the background of the parenting rules that were passed on to you. If your grandmother or great-grandmother was a part of the Greatest Generation, she lived through the Great Depression of the nineteen thirties. As a result, she may have suffered real poverty that affected how she was parented and then how she parented your mother or father or perhaps even you.

There is a cycle of modeling that occurs in all families, which imprints sibling behavior. You have to take a look back in time at our parents' hourglass and then go back another generation to their parents' era. This takes looking at something people in the field of aging call "cohort groups" or a "cultural generation." A cohort is sort of a shortcut way of expressing a whole era or time in history that deeply affected the people who lived in that epoch. Historians have given cohorts names to mark the historical passages through which these people lived. Here, five cohort groups from the twentieth and twenty-first centuries are analyzed that may affect the way you and your sibling relate today. These include:

- Greatest Generation
- Silent Generation
- Baby boomers
- Generation X
- Generation Y

Greatest Generation Cohorts and Siblings

Let's look at the first cohort that may have taught you or your parents how to parent siblings. If you are in midlife, your grandparents grew up in the Greatest Generation cohort. They were born within the first twenty-five years of the twentieth century. They were kids during the Roaring Twenties. The economy cooked until it burned out when they ranged in age from tweens to newly married young adults. In 1929, the Roaring Twenties—the high-flying American way of life— ended with the spectacular economic crash of the Great Depression. Due to this financial crisis, the Greatest Generation is also often referred to as the Depression Era cohort.

During the Great Depression of the nineteen thirties, the song "Brother, Can You Spare a Dime" became a constant refrain when the unemployment rate verged on 25 percent. In these desperate times, the economy may have buckled, but what held together was the family. Kin stayed as one tight knit unit as parents, brothers and sisters stuck to one another through thick and thin. And during the Great Depression, there was a lot of thin. Family was the center of the impoverished universe everyone inhabited. Fathers may have been out of work, but siblings worked when they could and many dropped out of high school to help feed their families. In this bread line economy, divorce was unheard of and stepfamilies happened only if children were given away due to their own parents' inability to feed and clothe them.

When World War II broke out, the American economy resurged, effectively ending the Great Depression. It was at this transition when the Depression Era Generation became what many know as the "Greatest Generation", a term for this cohort coined by legendary NBC news anchor Tom Brokaw. Young men from this generation joined the war effort *en masse*, and young women joined the workforce, supporting the war effort in factories or staying home and tending victory gardens.

The Greatest Generation can be summarized as having traditional values and a strong work ethic. Families were united by the cohort values of obedience and clear definitions of authority. Kin lived and died at home. There was little cash for entertainment, but people huddled around radios the size of modern day dishwashers to hear radio shows that offered distraction from the crushing outside world. Popular shows like *Fibber McGee and Molly* and family-centric shows like *Pepper Young's Family*, which portrayed a big nineteen thirties clan, spun out popular daytime radio dramas. These radio plays were all about folks getting through the economic tsunami of the Depression.

Silent Generation Cohorts

The cohorts of the post-WWII Eisenhower era, oftentimes called the Silent Generation, were born between the dawn of the Roaring Twenties and the years right before the breakout of World War II. Many were too young to serve in World War II, but their fathers and older brothers were recruited, fought and, in many cases, died during that conflict. In contrast to the Greatest Generation, many individuals from this generation came of age during a time of post-war economic affluence and a strong sense of patriotism. The suburban, nuclear family became the prominent depiction of American life.

It was during this generation that the "American way of life" was solidified. Consumerism blossomed during the Silent Generation. Many of these cohort members were scarred by the Great Depression and wanted to provide for their families in a way that their parents had not been able. Many of the young men in the Silent Generation fought during the Korean War and upon their return they entered into a booming and prosperous corporate work field and a newly suburbanized America. Climbing the corporate ladder emerged as the chosen path. For young women, career positions were attainable, but creating their own nuclear family remained a primary focus. Loyalty to the American way was expected; in fact, most people who came from this generation were quiet, conventional and happy members of the post-World War II corporate culture.

A modern depiction of a typical Silent Generation member is Don Draper, the popular main character in the television series *Mad Men*, who fought during the Korean War and came out of that conflict wishing to push himself into the world of advertising. Both his bizarre TV plotline experiences during the Korean War and his Depression-era childhood created the thematic crux of the Emmy Award-winning AMC series. *Mad Men* portrays this nuclear-fueled nineteen fifties world where men vaulted up the corporate ladder and moms stayed home and raised several children in an affluent cocktail-sipping, smoke-hazed suburbia. Kin was still the center of American life and the multiple siblings in large families were still taught to take care of one another. These fifties clans were hovered over by paternalistic dads embodied by Robert Young in the lead role of the 1954 television series *Father Knows Best*.

It is important to note that this generation was not altogether silent. In this time of peace and prosperity came the opportunity for many members of this generation to question societal values, effectively creating the framework for the next generation, the baby boomers, to permanently change American society.

Artists and bands who would later define the baby boomers were made up of members born to the Silent Generation, including members of the Rolling Stones and the Beatles as well as Frank Zappa, Jimi Hendrix, Janis Joplin and Bob Dylan. The Beat movement of the fifties, who were the precursors to the hippie movement of the sixties and the baby boomer tide, began during the Silent Generation through the emergence of such acclaimed authors and poets like Allen Ginsberg, Jack Kerouac and William S. Burroughs. One of the women's movement's most established figures, Gloria Steinem, was a member of the Silent Generation. The civil rights movement, which shattered all racial rules of the Greatest Generation and brought about a Supreme Court case that changed the face of education via the landmark *Brown v. Board of Education* ruling, began with Martin Luther King, a Silent Generation member and one of the all-time great American leaders.

Baby Boomer Cohorts

When World War II was won and the GIs streamed back into the United States, they made lots of babies and pushed the American birth rate up to record numbers. If you are a midlife sibling, you are likely a member of this generation. The baby boomer cohort is defined as those born between 1945 and 1964.

As described earlier, a bustling nation emerged out of the war industry into what became known as the post-Eisenhower economy, and the baby boomer infants came as a shockwave that filled maternity wards, then elementary schools that were built by the hundred thousands. By the power of their record births, baby boomers were about to remodel American society.

Given the large span of time attributed to this generation, some divide it into two cohorts. The first half of the baby boomers—those whose birth was between 1945 and 1954—were born into great prosperity and came of age in the revolutionary years of the nineteen sixties and early nineteen seventies. The second half of the baby boomer generation was born between 1955 and 1965. These individuals began life in a still-prosperous America. However, in contrast to their earlier cohort members, it was a society facing great cultural challenges and they came of age at a time when America was not able to deliver them the same level of benefits experienced by their predecessors. During the late nineteen seventies and the early nineteen eighties, the younger baby boomers faced a world of stalled opportunities and economic chaos—including the highest unemployment rates since the Great Depression.

It is during this era that cracks began to publicly emerge in the American sibling veneer. In spite of strong family ties and an almost-zero divorce rate during the Eisenhower fifties, baby boomer siblings started to pull apart. Since they had more affluent families, boomer kids didn't have to work extra jobs to keep the family afloat like Greatest Generation siblings. Baby boomer brothers and sisters were not taught to be as loyal to one another, as siblings in the Depression, who were schooled in family faithfulness, because relatives needed their loyalty to survive. The baby boomer family was not only surviving but also thriving, so siblings squabbled over the oldest getting more, the male child getting everything, the baby being the sickening favorite and the one whom Mom loved best. The sibling warfare of today was set up in this generation. Although most families still lived and died together, family members resided close to home and siblings generally got along with each other, a sense of entitlement and a belief that "it is all about me" evolved.

Ozzie and Harriet, the highly popular 1960s television show that spawned legendary heartthrob Ricky Nelson, was an excellent metaphor for the nineteen fifties baby boomer beginning. The television Nelsons were regarded as the quintessential American nuclear family. Mom stayed home and tended to young Ricky and older brother David. Dad Ozzie went to work as a bandleader and was the famous breadwinner. Ricky and David argued, but generally got along in their multi-bedroom Hollywood Hills home bought with postwar economic largess. The Nelson family home had all the upper-middle-class accoutrements for a calm, caring, solid, dependable childhood and a very sturdy nest.

But as baby boomer kids grew up, they started to turn the fifties world on its head. They were the most affluent generation of the twentieth century and also the most entitled. Greatest Generation parents had showered them with toys that they themselves never had in the dire straits of the nineteen thirties. Poodle skirts for girls and Davy Crockett hats complete with raccoon tails for boys were the trends. With their full pockets, Greatest and Silent Generation parents festooned their kids with Davy Crockett lunch boxes, watches, tracker knives, T–shirts and a wide variety of dolls. Every kid had stacks of 45 records and a record player on which to spin them. Their parents had the money because of a roaring postwar economy to buy their baby boomer children what they wanted. To put it simply, the baby boomers were coddled as children.

Many of these baby boomers became teens who radically disagreed with their parents' pro-war and race-based mentality. When faced with the Vietnam conflict, seeing the unsettling images of battlefields in *Life* and *Look* magazines, some took to the streets. Protests broke out all over the United States, exploding with demonstrating young boomers. There was a draft during the Vietnam War and many young adults were conscripted to fight in a foreign battle they thought was horribly wrong. "Hell no, we won't go" was the battle cry of many young men and women in the nineteen sixties.

Baby boomers focused on inner life rather than the outside achievement fought for by their Greatest Generation and Silent Generation parents. They sought spiritualism over science and self-gratification over the selflessness and drive of past generations. Where the Greatest and Silent Generations tended to be conformist, the baby boomers were centered on themselves and not drawn to following the pack.

Baby boomers and their children created a whole new genre in America that had never been present in the history of American society. This was a modern idea of the extended family. In the nineteenth century and the first third of the twentieth century, many aging parents or relatives lived with their children. The version of the extended family that evolved when the baby boomers started to have children was the extended family on steroids. This new baby boomer version of kin developed into multiple parents, stepparents, stepchildren, half siblings, stepsiblings, fictive siblings, plus vast numbers of grandparents and stepgrandparents.

Four stratospherically shattering societal changes marked the transformation of the family as the baby boomers started to have kids. Birth control, the women's movement, the rising female presence in the workforce and divorce shook the roots of the nuclear family to its core.

First, birth control pills were invented in the early nineteen sixties. Baby boomer teens could have sex without the threat of unwanted pregnancy, which in part set off the sexual revolution of the late nineteen sixties. Women could then choose how many children they would have or whether they would have a family at all.

Second was the women's movement. Many small but powerful women's movements, including the suffragists, had preceded the vast societal tsunami of the nineteen sixties women's liberation struggle. However, the sixties launched a crescendo of women questioning male authority and hierarchy. The highly educated women of the Baby Boomer Generation defied the patriarchal system that cast a cocoon around the family. Gender was the thread that controlled the network of kin, with dads being the priest-like leaders and sons being the dominant siblings. Women were subservient and female siblings were considered second class and the primary caregivers. All this was questioned in the women's movement along with the husbands being the dominant force in a marriage.

Third, the family value held sacred by the Greatest and Silent Generations was of women staying home and raising families. Women of the nineteen forties went to work in droves to support the war effort. Rosie the Riveter helped make bombers and supported GI Joe as he fought World War II. But Rosie gave up her drill and returned to the homestead when the soldiers streamed home and together they started to produce the prodigious children of the Baby Boomer Generation.

The daughters of these women primarily grew up within nuclear families and received solid educations financed by their affluent Eisenhower and post-Eisenhower era parents. These young women did not want to simply be housewives or secretaries; they wanted to use their educations to work at meaningful careers. While they did not put off childbearing like future generations will, baby boomer women became an important and soon-to-be required part of the American workforce in the nineteen seventies and nineteen eighties.

Finally, the specter of divorce loomed large over the baby boomer family and its Generation X children, who were born between 1966 and 1977. The divorce rate skyrocketed as well. Many women left unfulfilling marriages, rebelling against the constraints of matrimony and paternalistic structures. Baby boomer women blithely believed they could "have it all" —be single moms and raise their children.

Thus, the cataclysmic change in the extended family. The nuclear family, in which multiple siblings grew up in a safe little nest with Mom and Dad, was shattered. By the beginning of the nineteen seventies one in ten families in the United States was a single-parent family.

Generation X Cohort

The Generation X Cohort was very different from the past generations. They are children of the youngest members of the Silent Generation and the older baby boomer contemporaries. In comparison to their parents, Generation X members faced increased poverty as children. These children faced the same societal woes as the coming-of-age latter baby boomers. Largely because of rising divorce rates, single mother households became more commonplace by the end of the nineteen seventies. These single moms struggled with going back to school or working while juggling the burdens of childcare. Adding fuel to this economic struggle were the economic disasters of the 1973 oil emergency, followed by the energy crisis, the recession of the early nineteen eighties and the first imploding mortgage crisis. When the savings and loans scandal of 1987 imploded, it sparked the first wholesale bank bailout and further impacted the economy.

Oliver Stone's 1987 film *Wall Street* portrayed Michael Douglas as the hyper materialistic power broker Gordon Gekko, who wore designer power suits and slicked back hair and was consumed with himself and his stock-fueled riches and Charlie Sheen as his eager protégé. Meanwhile, young Generation X kids were finding the world was full of economic uncertainty, not the largess and security that their parents blossomed in as kids. Downsizing started to occur in American industry and giant plants closed, such as those in the steel industry and the auto industry. Jobs started to be outsourced overseas.

To deal with this bleak era, Generation X children were captivated by the sounds of heavy metal, grunge, punk, alternative rock and musical groups like Metallica, Nirvana and the Smashing Pumpkins, all expressing their sense of unrest and uncertainty mixed with anomie or hopelessness about the world they lived in. Generation X children withdrew into a celluloid world that mirrored their disenfranchised plight, including the films of iconic director John Hughes such as *Sixteen Candles*, *Pretty in Pink* and *The Breakfast Club*. They were at the same time the latchkey generation (named as such for the house keys worn around kids' necks), the MTV generation and the first generation growing up navigating the World Wide Web.

This shattered the family economically when it was already irrevocably changed culturally by divorce. As single moms struggled to support their children, more latchkey children evolved, because moms could not afford day care and were not home themselves to care for their kids. Broken families became more the norm and remarriages started to occur between recently divorced men and women, spurring the blended families within which Generation X children grew up.

Generation X siblings reacted to the strain of their parents in divorce, the depressed economy and the new tension of stepfamilies. Siblings were introduced as the stepsister or stepbrother, the new conundrum of the sibling relationships that would echo out into midlife during the early part of the twenty-first century. Generation X children strapped on backpacks and marched lockstep back and forth between their parents' homes. They had Mom's house and Dad's house, but no real home of their own. The nest that was so tightly woven against the cruel winds of the economic meltdown and was kept together by previous generations was blown to pieces for Generation X.

Television programs reflected several versions of this new Generation X family. The perfect nuclear family of the early nineteen fifties, like the one in *Father Knows Best*, evolved into many different versions of the family. One was the continuation of the nuclear family, but with a woman having an equal role, such as in *Roseanne*, in which a blue-collar family faced day-to-day economic privations. The woman in the family had a status equal to the man's and both family members had to work because of the difficult eighties economy. The model of the nuclear family was depicted on television at the time with *The Cosby Show*, in which the parents and siblings were upscale African-American New Yorkers. These siblings in these two disparate shows had their spats, but the parents interceded at every juncture and smoothed out the fights and the script. This particular scenario showed how the dad could still be in charge while the strong mother could hold down a high-powered professional career as well. Another template for nineteen eighties sitcoms was the single-parent family, oftentimes headed not only by a mom but by a dad, particularly *Diff'rent Strokes*. And while not officially stepsiblings, the Generation X children in *Who's The Boss?* grew up in a familial role reversal—a working mother hires a male housekeeper.

Generation Y
Born between 1978 and the early part of the new millenium, Generation Y is also known as the Millennial Generation. Characteristics

of the generation vary greatly, but generally these individuals have a heightened familiarity with a global economy and mass communications, especially digital technologies. Due to the various child-bearing patterns of previous generations, members of this generation can be the late-in-life children of the Silent Generation and the older baby boomer cohorts. Primarily however, these are the children of the younger baby boomer cohort and Generation X. Similar to the baby boomers, this generation can also be broken into two groups, those who were children in the nineteen eighties and came of age in the nineteen nineties; versus those who were children in the nineteen nineties and becoming adults after 2010.

Let's look at the evolution of the American family and the siblings who have lived in those families through the lens of the television camera over the last sixty years. Television showed America's different ideas of the extended family with many different types of siblings from the mid-seventies to the beginning decade of the twenty-first century. The role of siblings has been reflected in these television versions of the American family. Beginning in 1972, television viewers saw *The Waltons*, a classic example of the extended family Americans had known for generations. In 1974, viewers saw the family add the adopted sibling in *Little House on the Prairie*. In 1989, *Family Matters* provided a new version of the extended family, albeit much different from *The Waltons*. In 1990, *The Fresh Prince of Bel-Air* brought us an even newer version of the extended family. The television version of the family headed by the single mom evolved in the year 2000, with *The Gilmore Girls* and more recently, a small-screen version of Ron Howard's 1989 film *Parenthood*.

Although some families working within the nuclear form have hung together, the single-parent household is more the model for Generation Y. The parents of today's young adults may be compared to the dysfunctional movie parents of the blockbuster film series *Twilight.* Beautiful and lonely teenager Bella meets the ghostly, handsome Edward, because she has relocated since her parents' divorce to her dad's home in the rainy, dank town of Forks, Washington. This pack-your-suitcase moment comes because her immature mother has remarried a minor league baseball player and she sends Bella to her father so she can hobo around with her younger husband who makes a living playing a game. Bella feels like she is leaving her inept scatterbrained mom on her own to spend time with a dad she hardly knows. Edward, the paranormal, lonely boyfriend, has an intact, devoted and wealthy family—only thing is they are vampires.

Those who are "midlife siblings" and parents of "present-day siblings" need to learn and accept that their children are parented in families that are governed by many cultural rules passed on by generations past. Some of these are the rules parents learned from their parents and passed on to their children. To forgive a sibling who has hurt one long ago, enough to create an "I Hate You" story about the event, it helps to look at parents' rules and the historical and generational context of those rules. This will give the grace and the empathy to allow forgiveness on many levels and bring the sibling relationship back to a loving one. If you are a parent, you can look at rules you set for your sons and daughters and identify situations where children may clash among themselves and eventually, many years later, come up with an "I Hate You" story. The value of learning these lessons if you are a parent is that you can change the family rules passed on to your kids. This will help present-day families thrive and stop children from creating "I Hate You" stories in the future.

❧ Chapter 1 ❦

Define the
Sibling Relationship

Some siblings make music together. You can hear that genetic connection in such popular acts as Van Halen, Radiohead, Heart, Oasis and even the hip-hop group Clipse. What we listen to is that deep family relationship translated into a musical link. These brothers and sisters grew up in the same houses. All heard their parents' music and some started playing instruments at the same time. What we see is sibling connection: similar DNA translated into a creative musical splicing. Siblings have that same genetic song to sing, leaving auditory fingerprints for us to dance to and enjoy.

But that sibling connection can also sound like chalk scraping on a blackboard. Brothers and sisters sometimes suffer serious sibling rivalry. Creedence Clearwater Revival spun into chaos when older brother Tom Fogerty tried to dominate their music and younger brother John Fogerty rebelled. Their group fell apart and disbanded. When Tom died of AIDS from a blood transfusion in 1990, the brothers had never reconciled.

As embryonic sharks grow in their mothers' wombs, the biggest baby devours the rest of the young to make sure he or she has enough to eat. The first-hatched eaglet slays all new hatchlings by pushing them out of the nest, receiving all the food brought to them by the parents, thus ensuring his or her survival. The first recorded murder in history, the Bible tells us, was Cain killing his brother Abel. We all know the blood and gore accounts of myths, fables and even new stories chronicling the concepts of sibling rivalry.

What is a Sibling?

There can be brothers and sisters, brothers and brothers or sisters and sisters. Full siblings, born of the same biological mom and dad, are the most common form.However, we can also be siblings with one parent in common, which we call half siblings. Although the word "sibling" calls to mind a blood relationship, being a sibling is not just a matter of biology. A brother or sister connection can be made socially. It does take two or more children in a family to have a sibling. We can also say someone is a sibling and have no genetic connection. Stepsiblings are blended together through marriage, not through blood. We have adopted siblings, foster siblings, even something called fictive siblings, which is similar to that of a blood brother. Fictive siblings are accepted into a family through custom or just plain choice. Being a sibling is not just a bond of blood but also having some degree of common genes, common history, common family values and culture or legal status. Whatever the tie—blood, marriage or custom—it is our deepest bond in the family and almost 96 percent of us have at least one brother or sister.

Siblings are the longest thread through our lives. They are the most enduring relationship we ever have in our family. Many brothers and sisters create bonds when they are very young, albeit depending on their ages, differences and roles. Siblings usually go through pimply teenage misery with us, attend our weddings, then sometimes drift off as we marry, raise kids and come back to a closer relationship later. Often the most enduring bond as we grow old is that with a sister or brother.

Sibling Struggles from Childhood Through Midlife

On the other hand, for many of us the family roads we followed were rutty and, for some, the paths have encountered some gaping potholes along the way. At times conflicts between young siblings rupture the relationship. Because the damage done by a sister or brother can leave a deep gash, sometimes it never heals. In fact, that old wound from a sibling may still fester and ooze enough to lead us to say we still hate him or her.

We feel we hate our siblings for many different reasons. The chief complaint that lurks in our minds is that Mom or Dad favored them over us. She got the new prom dress for her high school celebration and a few years later we ended up with her hand-me-down. Dad sent him to a great four-year college and we were sent to a community college near home. She was the baby and got to grow up with late curfews and loose rules while Mom and Dad were unbearably strict with the rest of us. He was the oldest and Mom needed him to take care of the bunch of us, so she let him boss us around. She was the stepsibling who moved in and took over half the bedroom.

Seeing Siblings in the Second Half of Our Lives

Maybe you have a brother or sister to whom you hardly speak. Perhaps you see that sibling on holidays and largely ignore him or her or make do with superficial chitchat as you seethe inside. If you fit this description, you are in the same lurching boat as uncounted siblings all over the world. That wound from childhood may still ache enough to keep you on the furrowed journey your family followed when you were young. Now, however, you and adult siblings may need to come together again to be part of a niece or nephew's wedding or christening, help plan a parents' anniversary dinner or oversee the care of elderly family members.

Adult siblings often are brought back together at family events. The family stage is set up once more, but now the warring characters may be brothers or sisters who have their own families and lives. If the sibling breach has not been cauterized and is still stiffened like a coiled wound, the wedding, bris, communion or holiday feast can turn into high drama, ignited by emotional flashbacks from childhood.

When an adult brother or sister needs help from others in the family, this often slams siblings together again. It may be a serious illness, financial crisis, major depression or calamity. When family must team up to organize care, wounds from childhood can unsuture. The earlier spilled blood can prevent family members from giving the sibling in crisis the care he or she needs.

Siblings may be shocked out of sleep by midnight calls from brothers and sisters frantically telling them of a crisis with Mom or Dad. Adult children are often forced to book last-minute, high-cost airline flights and gather in scary, sterile hospital rooms with brothers and sisters to whom they have not spoken in years. Siblings might stare starkly at each other, then have to face doctors and social workers who may ask the family to make excruciating decisions about Mom and Dad.

At times some avoid going to see parents because of sibling wars. We want to avoid that sister who bossed us around when we were kids, because she is still telling everyone what to do. Or we want to deck the brother whom Dad pitted against us when we were boys. Every time we see him, he tells us how he's got more money and bigger cars and we can't stand having him at the family dinner table.

Those stepsiblings who entered your life when Mom divorced Dad and married again, destroying your warm family, are there at

Mom's birthday. You are still angry at them for ruining your family, draining away your parent's love, even though you know blaming them is easier than blaming Mom or your stepdad. Or the baby brother or sister you always knew Mom favored instead of you is going to be at the holiday dinner and you still say under your breath, *Mom loves you best and I hate you for it.*

Reasons to Reconnect

In spite of any longstanding issues or beef you may have with your sibling, in adulthood some of us want to reach back and repair those cracks in the familial foundation. We may want to be friends with our siblings and stepsiblings again, because deep down we really care for them in spite of the pain they may have inflicted upon us growing up.

Perhaps your stepbrother is getting married and his bride has asked your children to be flower girls in their wedding. You love your daughters and know they would glow in the spotlight, dressed as little princesses, haphazardly throwing roses down the aisle. But you suspect that dormant old rage may reactivate. To honor this occasion and please your kids, you think maybe the time for reconciliation is at hand.

You may know from your mom or dad's present level of mental confusion the worst is coming. You suspect it's important to repair your old wounds with your sibling so you can help your parent. You are searching for a way to forgive and in this guide we will be mapping out a step-by-step plan to forging a better relationship.

Forgiveness is Doable

Let's take the first step to getting on the path. Forgiveness is doable and making amends with your siblings is achievable. In this book, we propose a process that will allow you not only to forgive your siblings, but to forgive yourself as well. These ten stages will allow you to move toward exoneration, feel better about yourself, mend the past with your brother and sister and repair that pothole-riddled childhood road so you and your siblings can move into the future as a united family.

Here's how to phrase your pain on paper: First, express it out loud and then write your sibling story. It will help you move from the past to the present to soothe that hurt. We will give you the tools to uncover the family rules that instructed you and your siblings on how to behave. You will also have a chance to put yourself in your brothers' and sisters' places and see what led to such damage in the first place. As you take the steps we recommend and do the exercises suggested in this book, you will have the opportunity to expose the sibling wound of your youth to the present day and uncover how you and your brother or sister may still be hurting you.

As you unearth the pain you have lived through in regards to your sibling conflict, we'll reveal ways to make yourself healthy and happy. Using your positive feelings, you can tell your sibling your "I Hate You" story and give him or her a chance to understand your weary, sad feelings and then you can hear his or her side of the story. You can then "give peace a chance" and allow yourself to take the steps to reestablish a relationship.

Forgiveness can be just for you and does not always have to involve your brother or sister. We'll discuss how to make peace with yourself with or without an apology. If it does involve a sibling and he/she does apologize, we will reveal some steps you can take to accept that request for forgiveness. If your sibling says he is sorry, we will show you how to establish a new family relationship. Finally, using forgiveness and learning all the ways you can value yourself will show you how to put together a team relationship with your family. You can help plan a family reunion, teach your children to be full participants in family rituals, handle parental problems and really forge that new sibling relationship in your adult life that will lead to a fulfilling connection in adulthood.

What is an "I Hate You" Story?

An "I Hate You" story is something that happened between you and your sibling when you were younger that caused damage to you. In your mind the pain was caused by your brother or sister. As a result, you may think your mother loved your sibling more than she loved you. It could have made you believe your sibling did not love you at all. It could have given you the feeling that you did not love your own sister or brother. Perhaps this hurt turned into a story that has repeated in your mind over and over again.

You are now joining us on a journey that will allow you to tell your "I Hate You" story about your sibling. In reading this book and putting the suggestions to work, you will start on the path toward forgiveness. We believe this journey will help you feel emotionally and physically better and improve your relationship with your sibling and your family. Hopefully this path will allow you to gain insight into what happened between you and your sibling and to forge a closer bond in the future.

Perhaps you have young children or teenagers of your own. You may be worried that someday those kids will throw their own spears at each other with the battle cry "Mom loves you best." If you do not want to be that toxic mom or dad yourself and you want to avoid further scarring, here is important information for you to utilize. Now you will not carry the techniques and battle weapons of sibling warfare into your own parenting. Too many moms and dads re-create their own brother and sister issues with their children. In this way, kids may re-create historical parental conflicts. Our book will help you nurture your family in a way to assist your children in avoiding future wounding attacks on each other and aiding your kids to work together as a better team for the rest of their lives. We believe this book will also help you better parent your own kids and guide them to better sibling relationships.

Who We Are
We are professionals in the field of social work and have led many workshops on the problems brothers and sisters encounter. We have worked with many adult siblings who were angry with their brothers and sisters and have researched and written about sibling rivalries and issues. We learned that the antagonism many siblings feel toward each other comes from a pain deep down inside them, erupting from something that happened many years ago. They have avoided their brothers or sisters and do not feel good when seeing them, but have a hard time pinpointing where the hurt came from. You may be one of these people. You may also be a person who now wants to try to resolve the rift between yourself and your sibling. Many things can happen in our lives that lead us to think we want to make peace with a sibling. Next we'll consider some common reasons why you might want to change your "I Hate You" story. There could be many more reasons than are listed here.

Reasons to Help Change Your "I Hate You" Story
Here are some suggestions to help alter the trajectory of your sibling "I Hate You" story:
- You and your sibling see each other at family holidays and special occasions like weddings and funerals. When you are there, you do your best to avoid your brother or sister. You have been thinking you should do something about the negativity, but are unsure what.

- You are asked to help plan a family event or have your children participate in a wedding or some other type of family event. However, you are conflicted between your feelings of anger or resentment and the need to gather the clan together to celebrate an otherwise joyful occasion.
- You and your sibling are caught in a crisis regarding health or financial issues involving your parents and you have to communicate with all your siblings again. As a result, you must work with the brother or sister who caused your "I Hate You" story and your pain resurfaces.
- You have chosen not to see your sibling for years, but somewhere deep inside your heart you wonder what would happen if you tried to reconnect.
- You have attempted to be friendly with the sibling you don't like and it just has not worked out. However, now you'd like to give it another try.
- Members of your family have asked you to attempt to forge a better relationship with your brother or sister. You are willing to make the effort, but you are not sure about how things will turn out.

If you feel angry or resentful toward a sibling yet motivated to get to the bottom of that memory and perhaps change things, this book can help you do that. To begin, let's look at the origins of the bad memories revolving around your brother or sister. Perhaps you are also concerned that your own young children or teens may have contentious connections that will end in an "I Hate You" story. You want to learn what you can do to help your own young daughters and sons have loving relationships with one another.

Origins of an "I Hate You" Story
Let's consider how an "I Hate You" story starts. Something transpired in your past between your sibling and yourself that you did not wish to happen. As a result, damage was inflicted and the pain encapsulated like a cyst under your emotional skin. It is a wound that is covered up, but remains deeply held inside your mind. This hurt from your past may have turned into a story you have kept hidden or perhaps tell yourself and others over and over again whenever your sibling's name comes up.

Different People, Different Reactions
Sometimes siblings hurt us and we are able to let go of that pain: It does not turn into a wound that stays in our minds. But with some other brothers and sisters, that emotional injury turns into a psychic lesion that festers for years. If you are a person whose sibling wound has turned into an "I Hate You" story, we will be discussing what measures, realizations and steps will allow you to bring that encapsulated wound to the surface of your mind and expose it to the forefront. Doing this will permit you to see the real problems in your sibling relationship. Understanding your sibling story will:

- Give you insight into a sibling's past harmful behavior;
- Allow you to avoid being vulnerable to that behavior in the present;
- Help you protect yourself in future relations with siblings;
- Identify where you are stuck in your relationship with your sibling.

Other People's "I Hate You" Stories
You are not alone in your estrangement. Other siblings have suffered relationships that are strained and difficult. Here are some true experiences:

Ted's Story

Ted and his older brother, John, grew up with a single mom. Their dad abandoned the family when John was eight and Ted was six. The boys did not see him again until they reached their twenties. He left their emotionally overwhelmed and immature mother, then a single parent working as a salesclerk in a local dress store six days a week. She began to abuse prescription anxiety drugs, causing her to be out of touch with her family. After school, Ted was cared for by older brother John, who himself was emotionally confused and hurt by his dad leaving the family. The fun and freedom of after school activities ended for teenage John and he resented the burden of having to look after Ted.

One afternoon, Ted changed the television channel from John's favorite sports show to *Howdy Dowdy*. Furious, John went out in the back shed and broke some glass canning jars. He swept the broken glass in a circle and jammed a short stool in the middle. John marched back in the house, grabbed Ted, took him outside and sat him on the stool after yanking off his shoes and socks. John ordered Ted not to move until their mother came home then went back inside the house to watch his sports show. A short while later, John heard shrieks from the backyard and ran out to find Ted with his feet bleeding profusely, surrounded by two screaming neighbors. The women took Ted to the emergency room and called the boys' mother, who rushed to the hospital. Ted had to have ten stitches in each foot. The mom punished John, but since she needed him to watch Ted, she continued to leave John in charge. Ted never forgave John for the incident.

John grew up and became an FBI agent. Ted, meanwhile, became a social worker. Every holiday the family gathers at John's house. The older brother usually dominates the day, telling loud crime stories from his job where he is always the hero in between bossing around his wife and kids. Each time this happens, Ted tries to be friendly and understand his brother, but inevitably starts to seethe inside as the evening drones on. As a social worker, Ted feels he should love his brother and try to get along with him, but he always ends up with a knot in his stomach and feeling sick for a day after these family get-togethers. Ted has an "I Hate You" story about his brother John and does not know what to do about it. His brother is his only sibling and Ted wants to be his friend. But every time he sees John, he experiences both a mental and a physical reaction that leaves him feeling depressed and queasy.

Adult Siblings Facing Their "I Hate You" Story
If you have chosen to reconsider the origins of your "I Hate You" story, there is real hope that you and your sibling might become close again. The wonderful thing about adult sibling relationships is that their roles are ascribed rather than earned. No matter how much money you make or what hedge funds you manage, you can't earn being a sibling. You are siblings mostly because of your birth and the choices your family made. You remain a brother or sister for life no matter what. This unique quality really counts as you grow older. No matter what arguments have separated you or how many years have taken the wattage out of your relationship, a sibling bond can be lit up again, all because it never really goes away. It is part of your family heritage.

Ted has been angry for decades because he was deeply hurt by a sibling and that damage turned into a wound that festered inside his mind. At the center of this wound is something that happened in their childhood that they did not wish to happen. At the same time, something that they wished to occur never transpired. Ted wished for an older brother who would care for him safely when he was little. But when his brother was supposed to watch Ted, he instead harmed him physically. An "I Hate You" story starts because something happened that you did not want to occur and what you wished never materialized.

Ted's story shows us how hard it can be when there are issues of blame and hurt that exist between a brother or sister and ourselves. Many different things can happen with a brother or sister that can evolve into an "I Hate You" story.

Tammy's Story

Tammy was the youngest of five children and always her mother's favorite, making her four brothers and sisters jealous. Now that her parents are old and frail, she has taken the lead in caring for them. Tammy asks Paula, the middle child, who lives near Mom and Dad, to help with their parents' care. However, Paula feels Tammy got so much attention when they were young, her baby sister deserves to do all the work for Mom and Dad. Instead of helping, Paula routinely comes over and criticizes and snipes at the way Tammy does the dishes and makes the bed. Paula calls her other siblings and tells all her gripes about Tammy to them. The brothers and sisters then call Mom and Dad and complain to them about Tammy's care. Tammy feels like she hates Paula.

Angie's Story

Angie's mom died in a car accident. Soon after, her father married Jennifer's mother, which, in turn, made Jennifer and Angie stepsisters. Angie's new stepmother favored her own daughter over Angie, always giving Angie more of the chores at the house than she gave Jennifer. She told Jennifer how beautiful she was all the time, but never gave Angie the same positive feedback. Angie grew up never feeling she was pretty enough and really disliking Jennifer. Angie blames Jennifer for her negative feelings about her self-image.

Ginger's Story

Ginger cares for her mom, Pat, who had a stroke. She comes over every night after work and fixes dinner and leaves a lunch, then goes home to her own family. She has asked her brother, Bobby, to help, as he lives in the same town. He says that his work as a dentist is harder and more important than Ginger's, who is a secretary, so he can't help. He tells his sister he will call Mom on weekends, but that's about it. Bobby always got out of doing things around the house when they were kids, as Ginger remembers it. Mom criticized the way Ginger vacuumed, but never even asked Bobby to pick up the vacuum cleaner. Ginger is angry with Bobby now, just the way she was as a kid, and hardly talks to him when the holidays come around.

Daryl's Story

Brothers Mike and Daryl have always been pitted against each other by their parents. Their mom bragged that Mike got his first tooth earlier, walked earlier and was smarter in school. Daryl, who is younger than Mike, has always felt jealous of his brother. Now that they are adults, when Daryl sees Mike he's friendly, but he always feels tension in his body when his older brother is around. He knows the anxiety is deep down inside and related to his feelings about Mike.

Roger and Vera's Story

Stepsiblings Roger, Vera and Randy have found themselves living in the same house after Roger's and Vera's mom, Gayanne married Randy's dad, Amos. The three stepsiblings are at extreme odds with each other by virtue of their parents' divorces and remarriage. Randy must share a room with Roger. There is less household income due to three kids and the economic downturn; Vera can't buy the expensive clothes she craves on the Internet. Plus her mother has canceled the new mp3 player she promised. Roger has lost half his bedroom and storage for all his treasured toys like his building blocks and action figures. Roger also feels like he has lost his dad and has to share a bedroom part time with a stepbrother he hardly knows. These kids are on their way to an "I Hate You" story, and their parents and stepfamily are future cast members as the villains in the tales.

Jinx, Fess and Snookie's Story

Glenda and Oscar are a twenty-first-century couple who have been married for fifteen years. The twosome has three children of whom they are proud—Jinx, the oldest, Fess, the only son and Mary Louise, the baby, whom the parents have given a pet name, "Snookie." Mom Glenda works full-time as a nurse practitioner at the local hospital, working ten-hour shifts, four days a week. Dad Oscar is a contractor who has been under a lot of stress lately with the housing market slump. He has taken a second part-time job at a home improvement store in the hardware department. The parents are working hard to keep the family lifestyle intact, although they have had to cut back on many things like horse riding lessons for Jinx.

This has made Jinx miserable, as she loved her horse, Trigger, and she feels that her parents have been unfair by taking away her equestrian lessons plus the horse she really loves like a pet, while leaving her brother's archery lessons intact. A still hormone-confused teenager, Jinx has signs of cutting, showing her parents there is extreme stress in their family. She seems to be taking her frustration out on her brother and herself. Both parents are worried that they are facing a future "I Hate You" story.

There seems to be a sense of favoritism over Fess and Snookie. In fact they just bought Fess a brand new long bow and have taken him each week to Frank Farley Memorial Park, where there is an archery range. They have more time to do that since they are not attending Jinx's equestrian shows any longer.Glenda recalls being really angry at her own brother when her mom favored him over herself. Oscar always felt bullied by his older sister, Emily, and even now when she is asking him to help care for his mom. Glenda and Oscar do not want their children to have similar relationships.

Both Jinx and Fess are really jealous of little Snookie, who is fourteen months old. The older kids feel Snookie has been getting a lopsided amount of attention and almost no discipline. Essentially, thirteen-year-old Jinx and nine-year-old Fess think Snookie runs the house. Snookie has been walking for a month and persists on ravaging Fess's model collection, leaving the tiny pieces all over his room. Fess feels like he gets blamed for the mess and his dad makes him pick everything up when he comes home cranky and tired after work. Jinx loves Snookie unconditionally, but it eats away at her that she is no longer the only girl and center of attention. Jinx has the subconscious feeling that she has been abandoned. She loves her little sister so much she won't do anything to hurt her, but she has started to hurt herself, putting little nicks in her arms with her fingernails. She has bruises on her inner arms and when her parents ask about the marks, she says that she has fallen or that Snookie hit her.

This sibling contention is exacerbated by the parental struggle to support their household. Often Glenda gets delayed coming home, because she is not relieved by the nurse who takes over for her due to the hospital being so understaffed. She cannot leave her patients when they are in labor, so she often stays extra hours. Oscar is working two jobs and seems to come home only between shifts. So often the kids are left by themselves, bored and hungry, because they haven't gotten meals on time and are upset about their parents not being there.

The whole economic struggle has thwarted Glenda. She had a dream when she was a teen that she would grow up with the perfect family, Martha Stewart-style meals, accompanied by matching towels in the bathroom and bedding. When she was a kid, her mom shopped at a bargain store, because the family budget was squeezed and Glenda dreamed, as she waited in the housewares department, of herself in the future buying matching bedding, blankets, towels and dishes. The present economic downturn of the modern economy has caused her to shop for bargains once again.

Jinx and Fess's parents' absence has caused dissatisfaction, leading to fights in which the two oldest children have hit each other and locked each other out of the house. Snookie, who is at a babysitter's from eight to four, is dropped off at 4:30, but often Glenda is late and Oscar is working his second job, so caring for Snookie becomes Jinx's job. It is also her job to watch over Fess, who does not always follow her directions. Glenda and Oscar have punished Fess when Jinx reports this and, seeing it as ratting on him, he has retaliated by punching her. Secretly resenting this, Jinx wants to hang out with her own friends and is irritated that Fess never helps change diapers or feed Snookie dinner. Jinx sometimes leaves Snookie's diapers unchanged, as being a budding teen, she's busy on her cell phone or online and forgets about her sister. When her parents discover this, they yell at Jinx, making her all the angrier, often then taking out her frustration on Fess, because she can't hit her parents and won't intentionally hurt Snookie.

Both Glenda and Oscar understand that they have a problem with sibling rivalry amongst their children. As a nurse and a midwife, Glenda recognizes what stress a new baby can cause and is aware of family dynamics from a professional standpoint. She also has a younger brother on whom she often took her anger out, just like Jinx does with Fess. Her dad especially favored her brother and was ready to pay for any sport Glenda's brother wanted to play and all the expensive sporting equipment. Glenda was gifted in school and if not for the full scholarship she received to the university, she may not have gotten to attend college. She took out very expensive student loans that amounted to over $10,000 with interest by the time she finished her master's in nursing. Paying these loans back has fully impacted the family's finances, which are already exacerbated by the present dire economy.

Oscar's mom really favored his older sister, Emily, and he recalls how mad he used to get at her bossy ways. In fact, right now his older sister is demanding that he help with his eighty-year-old mom's care. Oscar feels bullied by Emily even now when she is asking him to help care for his sick mom. This young twenty-first-century husband feels it is all he can do to keep his own family afloat. He does not have the time, he laments, as he's working a second job to keep his family financially together and not lose their home to the present mortgage crisis. Both parents would like to know how to deal better with sibling rivalry, but they do not know how to approach their own children's problems.

Glenda desperately needs help. She goes to the human resource office of her hospital and gets information about their work and family program. She is put in touch with a counselor through them. The counselor helps her with Jinx's cutting issues by referring the family to marriage and family therapy. Glenda finds that her insurance will pay for late day care and she can leave Snookie in a second day care center. This is not ideal, but it relieves Jinx from extra babysitting for Snookie and makes sure there is not one more item for Jinx and Fess to fight about if Glenda has to stay late at work.

The counselor also makes other suggestions and proposes ways that Glenda can parent more successfully. One thing the counselor

GLENDA AND OSCAR'S GENOGRAM

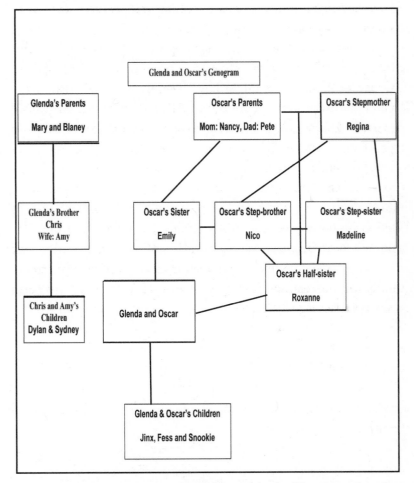

Glenda and Oscar's Genogram

| Glenda's Parents | Oscar's Parents | Oscar's Stepmother |
| Mary and Blaney | Mom: Nancy, Dad: Pete | Regina |

Glenda's Brother Chris Wife: Amy

Oscar's Sister Emily

Oscar's Step-brother Nico

Oscar's Step-sister Madeline

Oscar's Half-sister Roxanne

Chris and Amy's Children Dylan & Sydney

Glenda and Oscar

Glenda & Oscar's Children
Jinx, Fess and Snookie

recommends is to set limits carefully and fairly. The counselor also suggests that Glenda expresses these rules out loud to her kids, plus writes them down so they are a positive set of laws that tells everyone how to behave. Glenda starts by saying baby Snookie cannot have free reign to go into Fess's room and tear up his model creations. Fess's room is put off limits to Snookie; this rule is written very clearly in a document that is posted on the refrigerator and since the HR department has helped with emergency child care, Snookie won't be invading Fess's room when Glenda is not there to supervise her toddler.

These tales range from what appear to be relatively minor things to very serious situations that occur between siblings. But whatever the offences might have been in your own or perhaps your present younger children's or teens' situations, they have created "I Hate You" stories that have caused pain, but also made you feel that you might want to give peace a chance again. We would like to help you in doing this.

If you feel that you or your own young children or teens have an "I Hate You" story, we can help you tell that story. Next, we will tell you how to take the first step and get the brother or sister wound to surface from the deep reaches of your mind.

We believe that unearthing feelings and exposing them to the here and now can help you begin the work of forgiveness and re-forging better relationships.

❧ Chapter 2 ❧

Step Number One:
Put Your Pain on Paper

Adjusting the Shakespearian quote, our family is the stage. Parents and siblings are the characters on that platform, acting out our lives. As years go by, we become playwrights and recount the events on that stage through family stories. Most tales are good yarns, but in some stories bad things happen. Some of those unhappy memories about siblings become "I Hate You" stories. In this chapter we find out if you have one of those "I Hate You" stories and tell you how you can begin to heal from it.

Red Flags for an "I Hate You" Story

Researchers tell us there are several red flags that show us when we have one of these sad sibling tales.

Red Flag Number One

The first red flag which points to an "I Hate You" story is that you repeat your brother or sister story over and over, either in your mind or to others. Perhaps a parent or another sibling repeats the story and this frustrates you, causing you to think about the events again and again.

If you recount the same sibling tale time and time again, you do not have a memory disorder. All your memories are right there in your brain and some of him or her are very bad recollections.

Research tells us that siblings who are quite angry with another sibling and have intense, critical feelings about him or her usually have a fixation on their relationship.

In Angie's story, of which we spoke earlier, this repetitive element is present. Angie has a stepsister named Jennifer, whom her stepmother overtly favored. Her dad's new wife complimented her blood daughter Jennifer's hair, clothing and pretty smile, but stepdaughter Angie feels she was never paid the same compliments. Angie has very bad recollections of the time in her childhood after her dad remarried, notably of a new mother figure who was not kind or encouraging. Angie tells her husband and daughters this story repeatedly, especially when they are going to holiday events at her dad and stepmother's home or to other family gatherings where her stepmother and stepsister are present. Angie's teenage daughters like their Aunt Jennifer and grandmother and wish their mom would stop telling her childhood horror stories about them. They just want to have fun with their cousins and family. They really don't want to listen to Mom's old dramas. But Angie cannot forget the slights that resulted in deep hurts.

Angie tells these recollections over and over, because she is still in pain from the unhealed wound. Her "I Hate You" story has never stopped though it occurred long ago.

Red Flag Number Two

The second red flag that points to an "I Hate You" story is if something transpired in your recollections that you did not want to take place and you cannot forget the occurrence.

Remember Ted's story, which involves his older brother John? When they were children, John put Ted in a situation where he ended up with bloody feet, because he stepped on broken glass and then had to have twenty stitches. As a result, though his feet healed, Ted still has a wound inside his mind.

What happened to Ted occurred when he was a little boy. Although Ted's mom punished older brother John, she had to work and her eldest son was the only childcare provider she had. So even though John never physically injured Ted again, their bond was split, as if the broken glass had gotten under their skin forever.

Ted grew up in a family in which something occurred years ago that he never wanted to happen. As a result Ted stays clear of John as much as possible. On holidays when John swoops in and starts monopolizing the conversation, regaling the family with stories where he is the hero, Ted feels like running upstairs and hiding. He has an "I Hate You" story.

Red Flag Number Three

The third red flag which points to an "I Hate You" story is if you believe you are the victim in the story and your sibling is the scoundrel. You feel as though you were helpless while you believe your sibling had all the power. Your "I Hate You" story not only makes you feel like the injured party but also allows other   people who know you to see you as a victim.

Let's continue to use Ted as an example. Remember his antagonism toward his brother was seeded the day John got so angry that he set Ted on a stool outside their home, surrounded him with broken glass and walked off. Ted never forgot how he ended up in the emergency room and needed ten stitches in each foot and thus never forgave John.

Decades later, Ted still seethes inside when he's around his older brother. When he tells this story to his fellow social workers and his wife, John never ceases to be the villain and Ted is always the victim.

Ted is polite, but by the end of infrequent holiday dinners he is sick to his stomach and feels ill the next day. Every time Ted sees John, the mental and physical reaction leaves Ted depressed and ill. He feels helpless to do anything about this, as if he still was a little boy surrounded by broken glass. That is Ted's "I Hate You" story.

Red Flag Number Four

The fourth red flag pointing to an "I Hate You" story is if you continuously obsess about your sibling story.

Remember the story of Ginger, who cares for her older mom every day after work? As soon as she walks through her mother's door, she thinks of her brother Bobby. Although she has asked him for his help in caring for their mother, he has refused to offer Ginger any respite, even though he lives nearby. He says his work as a dentist is harder and more important than Ginger's secretarial job. Every single day when Ginger enters her mom's house to fix dinner, her blood pressure soars as she remembers her early and still-present anger at her brother. She thinks of how Bobby the kid, who got out of the chores she always had to do, turned into Bobby the dentist, who refuses to help with their mom's care. Ginger's doctor put her on medication and told her she needs to relax.

Red Flag Number Five

The fifth red flag common to an "I Hate You" story is based on different personality types of siblings. Let's find out which category into which your story falls.

Types of Siblings

Based on research that we have done on siblings, we have come up with six styles of relationships that exist between brothers and sisters. Choose the one you think fits you and your sibling.

- **Beloved Siblings**
  Beloved siblings care deeply about one another and see each other every day. They behave like best friends.

- **Buddy Siblings**
  Buddy siblings are like beloved siblings, but the caring between you is not as deep. You don't see them regularly, but you really like them. They are not your best friends.

- **Reliable Siblings**
  Reliable siblings are close, but usually live far way. You do not see or make contact with them frequently. However, you have strong family bonds and this sibling connection can be clamped into place in a family crisis and then released when things go back to normal. Reliable siblings are like air mattresses. They can be blown up and utilized at any time.

- **Listless Siblings**
  Listless siblings have little interaction with one another as adults. You are indifferent to each other. If there was a traffic light for siblings, it would be the blinking yellow light. You do not show much interest in him or her and are not sure exactly how the sibling feels about you. You suspect something happened in your past to make you so uninvolved.

- **Seething Siblings**
  Seething siblings are full of anger. You have a sense of hurt from childhood from a sibling that you feel deeply. You ignore him or her and don't have much contact except perhaps on required holiday visits. You are not physical

with your anger, but it sometimes seethes inside of you. Brothers and sisters who experienced strong sibling rivalry with no violence are in this category.

- **Irate Siblings**
  Irate siblings have a problem with a sibling about something that happened when you were younger. It may have involved aggression or violence. The story of Cain and Abel from the Bible is a good example. Brothers and sisters who experienced sibling rivalry can fall into this category if violence and aggression came into play.

Red Flag Number Five is waved if you believe that you and one of your siblings are one of the last three types— Listless, Seething or Irate—you probably have an "I Hate You" story.

Even as a listless sibling, an "I Hate You" story might exist subconciously. Uninvolved or listless siblings can still have extremely negative feelings toward a sister or brother. The lack of contact and involvement may be masking an incident that happened a long time ago, quelling the hurt or anger you feel and the story you are suppressing. This may make you indifferent to your sibling. A listless sibling thinks about the sibling and feels something is the matter, but can't pinpoint the reason.

If you are a seething or irate sibling who lives with deep-seated pain from childhood or even adulthood and have little interaction with your sibling, you might have an "I Hate You" story.

If you have a deep dislike of one of your sisters or brothers, which may have been caused by aggression, violence or sexual abuse, you are an irate sibling and surely have an "I Hate You" story. Even if you have any of these three sibling relationships, you can figure out the real meaning of the problems that exist at the core of your sibling story.

Finally, if you are a parent of young children or teens whom you feel exhibit sibling rivalry issues, you can help prevent your children from writing their own "I Hate You" stories. Through your guidance you can assist your own kids in expressing their feelings toward each other before they get to a listless, irate or seething sibling category to which they create a sense of animosity for one another that could haunt them and you for decades.

Jinx, from Glenda and Oscar's case study, has a serious sibling rivalry issue with her brother Fess. But her "I Hate You" story may go deeper because of jealousy in regards to new baby Snookie and deep psychological issues that have shown up in her possible cutting behavior. This sibling needs one-on-one counseling to tell her "I Hate You" story, which her parents arrange right away.

Fess, her brother, has an "I Hate You" story also, but the mom and dad choose to allow him to tell his story in a family meeting they convened. Glenda and Oscar hold a family meeting so that both of their children, who have been fighting nonstop since Snookie was born, can tell their sides of their embryonic "I Hate You" stories.

If you are a parent with young children, encourage them to tell their "I Hate You" story in different ways (see Relaxation Exercise for Teens and Children). One-on-one counseling is a good choice for children and teens who may have deeper emotional problems. Young siblings who are just at war with each other can tell their stories to a parent or family member, if they choose to do this, or in a family meeting where everyone's side of the story can be heard.

Telling Your "I Hate You" Story

Now we are ready to begin step number one of our "Sibling System for Forgiveness" and put your pain on paper. To take this first step, here are the tools to write your story and tell it to someone else. This will bring your wound to the surface.

Researchers have found that telling your story among kin, sometimes called reminiscence, can heal old wounds. Telling your story out loud or reminiscing with siblings can be the first step in healing long-festering lesions that exist in your mind. Researchers believe that doing life review as the years pass can help to end old battles with family members. When you can bring an old hurtful sibling into the "here and now," you can use the light from the present to begin forgiveness.

A review of your life can allow you to unearth stories in which something hurtful happened that you do not wish your own children to repeat. Research shows that telling your story can also help you put your emotional life in order to help you to feel calmer and less angry about childhood experiences. Telling your own raw story will not only free you, but also protect your children from the same sorrowful fate. It can give you insight into harmful behavior that may wound a family member in the future by repeating the same behavior. What you will learn from your story and what we will teach you in subsequent chapters can become knowledge and wisdom you can transmit to your children.

Finally, no matter what your age, research tells us there are four parts to completing relationships. These are:
- Asking and accepting forgiveness
- Conveying gratitude
- Expressing love
- Saying goodbye

You and your sibling may have forty or fifty years left before you die. Reflecting on earlier parts of your past together now may enrich the longest relationship of your life with decades of new support and friendship.

Writing Your "I Hate You" Story

Let's take a look at how to start to tell your sibling your "I Hate You" story. First, we would like you to practice a relaxing exercise for a few days. This technique will help you unwind and assist you in telling your story.

Find a place that is very private and where you feel comfortable. It could be your garden, a sheltered place in a favorite park or your own bedroom—any place that is quiet and allows you to be contemplative. After you find this location, go there and sit quietly. As everyone loosens up in different ways, you need to choose an exercise that helps you personally. Here is a suggested exercise that you can use.

Sit with knees tucked underneath you, arms out and palms facing up and let your eyes close. Bring your attention inward. You may want to nod your head gently from right to left, easily and slowly with your attention around the lower back area. Listen to the messages of comfort and discomfort that your body is sending to you. Continue to breathe deeply, because breath is the bridge between the mind and the body.

Focus on your breathing, beginning by taking full, deep belly breaths in and out through your nostrils. As you inhale, fill in your belly as if you have an imaginary balloon in your stomach. When you inhale, your belly expands out like a balloon as if it was inflating. This way the lungs can fill more fully. When you exhale, just let that imaginary balloon deflate and gently squeeze your bellybutton in towards the spine emptying out the lungs, making room for the next breath. Inhale, filling the belly and lungs with air; then exhale, allowing the belly to lower. Now continue this belly breathing at your own pace. You may want to place one hand on your belly, so you can feel the rising and lowering of your abdomen. You can feel the breath moving in and out of the body like ocean waves move in and out from the shore—so, too, does your breath… move in and out from your body.

Unclench your teeth; relax your jaw and tongue. Relax the muscles around your eyes and have a pleasant look on your face. Take the tip of your tongue and gently touch it to the roof of your mouth just behind the two front upper teeth. This is an energy point and it helps you relax all the muscles around your neck, your jaw and your face. But if this isn't comfortable, that's okay, just make sure you keep your teeth unclenched.

Now bringing your breath back to normal breathing, gently begin to wiggle your toes and fingers. Try to keep outside thoughts and distractions out of your mind. If they come in, gently let them out.

When you have practiced this relaxation technique or one you choose yourself for a few days, you are ready to begin to tell your "I Hate You" story. First of all, bring a pen and paper and sit down in that private, comfortable place you chose. Make sure you are alone and have a surface to write on, like a book, desk or clipboard. Relax and try to clear your mind. Use the relaxing techniques you have practiced.

After you feel yourself unwind, go back through the past in your mind and recall the painful experience that involved you and your sibling. Hold out your unclenched hands and slowly extend and relax your fingers, bringing those painful events to the surface. As you recall the hurtful incident, pay attention to how you are feeling. Do your hands want to clench again in fists? How is your breathing? Did it increase? Has your heartbeat sped up?

Now, take some more deep breaths, then pick up the pen and write down your painful story as you just recalled it. All you need is one or two paragraphs, but allow yourself to write more if you feel the need to do so. Like dreams you sometimes have before you awaken, if you write this down immediately, you can look at the story later and start to figure out what it means.

Telling Your "I Hate You" Story to Someone Else

To resolve your "I Hate You" story, you must now take a second step. Re-read your "I Hate You" story and think about a close friend or family member you really trust and who would gladly hear your story. For example, Ted might tell his wife or very close colleagues. Ginger might tell her best friend or someone from her quilting group.

When choosing a person with whom to share your "I Hate You" story, look for a friend or family member who has these qualities:

- You trust him or her.
- The person respects you.
- He or she will allow you to tell your story without interrupting.
- The person is a good listener.
- He or she harbors the ability to treat you like an adult.
- The person is willing to listen to your story without giving you advice.
- The person is a caring parent or counselor if the person telling the story is a younger child or teen.

After you have chosen this friend or family member, go over this list of qualities and what you will request when you tell your story. Ask if you could meet in private to tell your hurtful story to him or her. Make arrangements to get together within the following week of writing your story, if possible. Tell the person that although this is a first baby step toward forgiving your sibling, it is an important step. When you meet, bring your handwritten story. You may read it aloud or just tell it to this trusted person, just as you may tell it to yourself over and over again.

After you tell your story, you are ready for our next step, which is to bring you out of the past into the present. Forgiveness starts with you, so here is how to move away from your past and find ways to soothe your hurt in the present.

Helping Your Young Child or Teen Tell His or Her "I Hate You" Story

If you are a parent today struggling with a potential "I Hate You" story, write your child's or teen's budding sibling conflict story down so you can devise strategies to stop it from being an "I Hate You" story in the future.

Let's take a look at how to help your child or teen tell you his or her "I Hate You" story.

First, we would like you to practice a relaxing exercise with your young child or teen for a few days. This technique will help your child relax and feel more comfortable in telling you his or her story.

Parents can help kids learn to deal with thoughts and feelings as they arise and share their siblings issues with Mom or Dad. We can act as a mediator and help siblings settle their differences before they become "I Hate You" stories. You can do this with both warring siblings separately and privately, at different times.

We have made available a meditation to make space for angry feelings your teen or young child may have about his or her siblings.

Second, coming to peace with what is arising inside the minds of teens or young children helps them let these agonized feelings be felt and experienced, rather than getting stuck and cemented in their hearts, creating future "I Hate You" stories.

Find a place that is very private and where you and your child feel comfortable. It could be his or her bedroom—any place that is quiet and allows your child to be contemplative. After you agree on this place, go there and sit quietly. As everyone loosens up in different ways you need to choose an exercise that helps your child personally. Here is a suggested exercise that you can use.

Relaxation Exercise for Teens and Children

Ask your child to let his or her eyes soften or close. Invite the child to get in touch with his or her body...exploring what he or she is feeling right now. Ask him or her to move from the tips of the toes to the top of the head and out to the fingertips. Ask your child to get in touch with his or her breath. It may help to put a hand on the belly and feel the gentle rise and release of the breath with each inhalation and exhalation. Allow whatever feelings arise to be there, without trying to change them. For example, "I am feeling angry right now, helpless, frustrated or sad." Just be with whatever is arising inside the heart and mind.

Allow the feelings to be present, without needing to change them, make them go away, repress them or rage about them—just being there.

Once you have completed this meditation with your child or done a similar exercise that makes you both feel comfortable with your feelings, ask the child if he or she could share any anger about his or her siblings with you—the parent. Then have your child write the feelings about his or her brother or sister down in a notebook, diary or journal, if you choose.

·⁊· **Chapter 3** ·⁊·

Step Number Two: Be in the Here and Now

Now that you have brought your "I Hate You" story to the surface and have moved into the here and now, work on staying in the present. What is the advantage of staying in the moment? That's where the hurt and ache from your sibling story resides. Your body is always in the present although your mind catapults from past to present to future and back again, sometimes getting mired in the past. We want you to be able to feel healthier and resolve your painful sibling tale in the here and now. How do you do that? You already took the first step by bringing your "I Hate You" story to the surface and telling it to someone trusted. At this point, we need to move to step number two in our "Sibling System for Forgiveness" and be in the here and now—to move from the past to the present.

The present is really the only time we can change ourselves. The past is gone and does not exist except in your mind. The future has not happened yet and can only be programmed in your brain. But you can change the present and this is the reason to be in the here and now.

Ascertaining Your Feelings about Your Sibling

Think about how you now feel about your estranged brother or sister presently. Move from the past where you unearthed your old family pain and bring yourself into the current moment. Think about the last encounter you had with your brother or sister. This could be an actual face-to-face occasion, a phone call or an e-mail. Your sibling does not even have to actually be in contact with you. Recall an occasion that prompts a bad brother or sister memory.

In earlier chapters, we brought up some examples of such memories. Ginger drops by her aging mom's house every evening to help out. As soon as she walks through the doorway, she feels angry. Her blood pressure rises as she thinks of her brother Bobby and how he never helped her with anything. Weary, she walks into the kitchen angry about Bobby never helping with the responibilities for their sick mom.

Focus on Your Feelings in the Present

To focus on how you feel about your estranged sibling in the here and now, sit down in a place where you feel comfortable and can relax. Recall the last time you saw the sibling from your "I Hate You" story. What was the occasion? How did you feel when your brother or sister did something to remind you of what set off an explosion of hurt feelings? Remember the encounter does not have to be in person.

Whatever you felt when you had some present contact or memory of your sibling, write it down. A few sentences will do. Next, call your trusted friend and make a date to meet with him or her. This person is your partner in helping you enact change. Tell the person how you felt when you actually saw or recalled your brother or sister in the here and now as opposed to the past of your "I Hate You" story.

Caring for Yourself: What It Takes

Once you are on the edge of that sibling chasm you need to take steps to close this big gap by healing yourself.

In chapter 2, you checked off red flags that revealed you had a sibling story from your past. In this chapter, we focus on the ways you still are disabled presently when you encounter your sibling. Next, we want to soothe that pain by teaching you how to care for yourself.

Moving to Mindfulness

Change can really only happen by changing yourself. Clinicians tell us that in order to shut down the past you must close the book on this agonizing sibling tale. To do that you must first change the way you care for yourself.

How do you do that? You have already taken the first step. In this chapter, you moved from the past, where you were in pain, into the present. In the here and now you told your "I Hate You" story to a trusted friend. Now you are ready to take the next step. Instead of being stuck in the past where there is a wound festering underneath your skin, you need to dig at that lesion, get the infected tissue out and stitch it up. You have to work to heal yourself.

Begin with a concept called mindfulness. This means to be present in the moment while being purposeful and without judgment. You need to attain this quality to be a healthier and happier person.

Many family physicians have worked on mindfulness so they can avoid burnout and depression. Physicians are taught how to care for themselves and set boundaries and goals. Physicians do this to be better doctors. We are going to teach you to be a better caretaker of yourself.

Another group of people who need to utilize mindfulness are parents. To soothe a child, be it physically or emotionally, Mom or

Dad needs to be right there, paying total attention to the upset child in the present situation.

We have already taken a few steps to focus moving to change yourself. In chapter 2, we gave you a relaxation technique to help you unwind and bring your past "I Hate You" story to the surface. Now, we want you to use this same technique, but focus on how you feel in this very moment, not how you felt in the past.

Revisit the relaxation exercise we went over. Find a private place where you feel comfortable and safe. After you feel yourself unwind, recall the last time you saw, spoke, e-mailed or texted your brother or sister. How did your body feel when you were in this situation? Did you feel physically tense and ill at ease? Did your mind feel anxious?

Perhaps, as you sit in your contemplative space recalling your last contact with your siblings, you feel depressed, tired, angry, impulsive and hopeless; whatever the negative feelings you expose, these symptoms need to change in the present. To banish these symptoms you need to change yourself. In the end, you are the only person who can get rid of these present negative feelings. How do you do this? We are going to work on teaching you to care for yourself in this very moment so you can begin to heal your own wound.

Let's pretend you are your own caregiver. Your body and mind are in need of your own healing touch. Caregivers, like a mother or a father, can help nurse children back to health by soothing them, putting wet washcloths on fevered heads or reading stories to them. Let's soothe you.

Identifying Five Activities to Begin Healing Your Pain
If you have an "I Hate You" story, you are now paralyzed in the here and now. We would like you to choose five ways to help you begin to get rid of these negative feelings that have lingered in your

mind for a long time. You need to do this for that person inside you who is hurt from a long ago sibling rift. What we want you to do is begin to banish these negative feelings and replace them with positive feelings in the here and now. This involves action—moving into a positive activity that will help you heal and give you a more positive spin on your life.

What are some prescriptions or choices to give yourself as a caregiver in order to help yourself? Here are a few ideas from which to choose.

First consider some therapeutic activities therapists might suggest:

- **Massage:** At times the tension of an old relationship just lives in our muscles. Massage is a means of relieving those tensions. Your "I Hate You" story may have you in knots in the here and now and the best way to get rid of this is to have an expert rub it out. Massage also offers the human touch, the soothing washcloth of a caring person when we are in pain. This may be one choice you might make.

- **Journaling:** Have you ever kept a diary? Or have your ever maintained a calendar of events with some notes attached? This journaling can be as simple as that or as involved as purchasing a diary or keeping a journal on your computer. It is like a secret person with whom to share your thoughts.

- **Exercise:** This is an excellent way to help take care of the pained person inside. Let's consider the next self care choice you might want to do. Just walking every day can help you breathe a little better, give you a needed workout and let you see the life you miss by being sedentary. If you belong to a gym or have thought about joining one, now may be the time. Exercise can help expel negative feelings and increase the brain chemicals that make us feel more positive about ourselves.

- **Socialization:** Plan a dinner with a person you love in your family—a beloved buddy or reliable sibling or your own child. Connecting with amicable family and friends can be a really affirmative experience. It can remind us why we love our clan, why family is so important to our good mental health and how we warmly connect with family members or friends.

- **Meditation:** Today this can be available in the workplace, in your gym or in your community. This Eastern technique can help you learn to relax and help your body to be healthier and happier whatever your age. In addition your breathing can be more modulated, assisting stress issues and even health concerns like high blood pressure.

Identifying Five Activities that can Help Young Siblings Begin Healing Pain

Make a list of the five therapeutic activities you would like to start to better care for yourself in the here and now. Remember you have to do this before you approach a sibling when you are mired in an "I Hate You" story.

If you are a parent of a teenager or young child, help your son or daughter choose five activities that might help with his or her nurturing. Teenagers are perfect diary keepers and are so computer literate they can do this easily. High-energy kids of any age are naturally open to exercise, so engaging your children in new activities and sports that they like is a good way to take care of them and interact with them yourself as a parent. Driving them back and forth to activities gives you alone time with your children, even if it does stress your busy schedule. Remember, the end point of all this is to have healthier and happier children who have less stress with their siblings or stepsiblings. Socialization may include having more family gatherings that involve your parents and their grand-parents if they live nearby. The sense of family and a healing ex-tended family is what you are trying to work toward healing sibling relationships. It means encouraging any healthy socialization that your children crave, which might mean driving to more birthday parties, joining more school activities like wrestling, sewing, knit-ting, band or whatever else your children are willing to join. This also means more time on your part as a parent, but it will help you nurture your child and will move him or her toward self-worth.

As a parent of a teenager or young child who may be struggling with future sibling rivalry and dysfunction, avoiding your child's future "I Hate You" story may involve you yourself enrolling in ac-tivities that can help you take care of your own self. This will assist your child in moving through the shoals of sibling boundary issues. You, as a parent, might choose yoga, massage, journaling, medita-tion or increased socialization. Mindfulness could be a practice you investigate. Taking care of yourself as a parent and caregiver is key to looking after others. Young children who have brother and sister issues demand time and attention from you, the parental caregiver. Your first job is to care for them, but you cannot do that if you are not emotionally strong and centered yourself. Getting to that point means caring for the caregiver and using the appropriate tools to make yourself the best parent or stepparent you can be. You can help yourself achieve that by making a list of activities you can carry out to help your child or children.

Young Siblings Jinx and Fess Make a List of Five Activites
Siblings Jinx and Fess, who have been in a constant spat since baby Snookie came on the family scene, are assisted by their parents and

counselor in making a list of five activities they would like to begin.

Parents Glenda and Oscar realize that their kids desperately need activities after school. Both are home alone when they get off the school bus at the end of the day. Their sibling quarrels increase when there is no parent to intercede and set boundaries. After-school activities are a must for these clashing kids. However, the parents realize it may help Mom and Dad, but won't assist their kids unless it is an activity they want to do. Parents can't force kids to do activities the mother and father want them to perform.

Fess's parents are practicing this technique. When Fess feels stumped, his parents step in to help guide him. Their preteen has said in the past that he's really interested in archery, so his dad buys him a long bow. But he needs parental assistance to get involved in this sport. Father Oscar, who understands that his two kids are really stressed, decides to stretch himself further as a parent and make time to take Fess to archery practice. There's a local archery range in the county park near their home, and Oscar agrees to take Fess once a week on Sunday, when he's not working. He also puts up an archery target in the backyard. This is an activity that Fess decides to do right away. However, this makes the parents even more eager to have after-school activities, because they don't want Fess and Jinx home alone with a bow and arrow. Glenda discovers that the local YMCA has an archery club that meets one day a week after school. Fess agrees to sign up for it.

Fess needs to spend more one-on-one time with his dad, as he is frustrated about losing his favor as the youngest child to new baby Snookie. Archery is a new activity which meets that need. Encouraged by his parents, Fess says he would also like to go to Boy Scouts again. He had to give it up when Oscar did not have the time to take him between two jobs and a new baby. A frustrated Oscar talks to the scout leader, who is a mom, to work out some kind of a schedule. She offers to pick Fess up after school, along with her own son, the one day a week the scouts convene and take him to the meeting at her house. Oscar agrees to transport Fess to Boy Scout events on the weekends. Fess also will be signing up for Little League again in the spring and tells his parents he might look into basketball and chess club, held at school in the fall. So the strained sibling Fess has found five activities supervised by his parents that can help him have the one-on-one time and supervised after-school time. These activities will help Fess feel better about himself since the baby in the family took his place as the youngest, special child. This may really help with the sibling rivalry issues between him and his sister.

His sister Jinx is already seeing a counselor about her possible cutting issues. Mother Glenda needs to stretch in order to help her daughter, Jinx, who has many sibling issues with both her brother and the new baby. Trying to add other emotional outlets in Jinx's life, Glenda decides to visit the high school counselor to look for a less expensive school activity to replace the canceled horseback riding. The school counselor tells Glenda that Jinx might be interested in the drama group as she has a good friend who is in many plays. Jinx agrees to try this, but she exhibits more of an interest in working backstage with scenery and lights. Play practice is four days a week when a play is being produced, which is four theatrical events during the school year. She loves technology and art, and this seems like a good combination for her. The drama group, meanwhile, meets four afternoons a week when there is no play in production. This covers after-school activities for Jinx. It also gets her involved with many loners like herself. Jinx isn't Goth, but she loves black and sees herself as her own person. The drama group is like sweet and sour pickles. It produces great plays with kids who vary from cheerleaders to "at risk" students who wear black and are having trouble in school. It seems a perfect combination for Jinx's activity needs right now, her mom and dad decide.

Glenda, although overwhelmed by two jobs and a baby, understands from Jinx's counselor that she may have a future parental version of an "I Hate You" story with her daughter. One way Glenda can help to avoid this is to be more involved in Jinx's life. So Glenda, who has sewn all her life and taught by her own mother, decides to volunteer to make costumes for the plays as a way to support Jinx in the drama group. She can do it late at night when everyone is in bed. The counselor says in her one-on-one therapy sessions each week they should try to work on other activities. This might help Jinx feel better about herself in the here and now and develop her own self-worth, which may play a part in alleviating her cutting behavior.

Parents Need to Care for Themselves

If you are a mom or dad of younger siblings who are under stress and arguing among themselves, you are most likely experiencing a great deal of pressure and strain yourself. This may mean you would benefit from starting an activity to take care of your own well-being. You are the caregiver, one of the prime roles that parents have in nurturing siblings and making them successful brothers and sisters and caregivers need to take care of themselves.

Gayanne is a mother whose children, Vera and Roger (from chapter 1), have had serious problems that reached the breaking point when Roger had to go to the emergency room with an arm wound from a shoving match with his sister. Gayanne and Amos take the first step in helping themselves as caregivers by going to counseling.

When Gayanne starts counseling, the therapist recommends many steps to help this young mother and her current husband solve the sibling problems they are experiencing with their children. One suggestion is that Gayanne herself start a mindfulness class for stress reduction that is offered through the local hospital. Gayanne has shown signs of high blood pressure, so she agrees to enroll in the class even though it will stretch her budget all the tighter. She does not want to end up with a second divorce, kids with an "I Hate You" story and having to take blood pressure medication for the rest of her life. Plus, she wants to follow the direction of the counselor to reduce the fighting between her daughter and son. She also needs to integrate stepson Randy into the sibling mix, and this has stressed her out even more.

Glenda and Oscar Seek to Repair Their Family

Let's look again at Glenda and Oscar who are nuturing their aptitudes as caregivers as well. They have one child who has exhibited signs of cutting. The two older siblings are angry at the introduction of a new baby, who in their eyes has since become the favorite. This has put strain on the entire family system, which these young parents need to relieve. But to heal their children's wounds the midlife parents need first to care for themselves.

Glenda and Oscar have been married fifteen years and the strife between their children has really rocked their marriage. They have not had a sexual relationship on a regular basis and find themselves arguing frequently. Glenda is putting in a lot of overtime at work and is exhausted. Oscar has had to take a second job and is weary when he walks in the door. When they start seeing the counselor about what to do to help Jinx with her cutting issues, the counselor says that the problem is partly an overall issue of family dynamics. The mom and dad cannot absorb the constant worry and nervous tension of their arguing older children plus a toddler. The therapist emphasizes that they are the platform for the whole family and it will collapse if they do not care for themselves and their own marriage.

The therapist suggests that they look into marriage counseling after hearing of their own arguing and sexual issues. The way parents solve disagreements sets a strong example for all children and especially teens, she advises. As this family has a preteen and teen, the counselor reminds them that it is essential for this couple to work through disagreements in ways that are respectful, productive and in no way aggressive. With the number of sibling issues they have in their family, these parents need to set a model to avoid future sibling battles amongst their kids. The couple then decides to look into a marriage revitalization through Marriage Encounter in their local city. Their counselor tells them that this is a low cost program, which is very important to this financially strapped family. It is multidenominational and this appeals to both Glenda and Oscar. Being that the program is designed for couples in many situations, this mom and dad can separately be in counseling for their daughter while attending the marriage regeneration for themselves. Glenda and Oscar can work on their own marriage to strengthen their ability as a couple to help their daughter and son, who are all under stress. So they will be caring for themselves, something key to helping siblings who are perhaps facing future "I Hate You" stories.

These marriage encounter seminars occur on weekends, which poses a problem for the discontented couple. What will they do with their three children, especially baby Snookie? Glenda decides to call her parents, who live about an hour away and ask if they can come and stay with the three kids on the weekends when the Marriage Encounter sessions occur.

This means opening up to Glenda's parents about Jinx's problems and her own marital troubles. But the counselor they are seeing for Jinx's mental health says that one of the best things a family can do to help problematic siblings is to reach out to extended family. They decide to take her advice.

Glenda has not had a great relationship with her parents and they have not always willingly helped her out. They are caught up in the activities enjoyed in their own retirement, like golf and acting as docents at the art museum and seem to pay more attention to Glenda's brother's kids, who live nearby.

This is a very sore spot for Glenda, because she feels that her parents always loved her brother best, although she suspects she may have repeated this pattern with her own family. When she makes the call, both her mom and dad readily agree. A weekend is set up when Glenda and Oscar can go to Marriage Encounter and Glenda's parents will take the three children. This gives the worried parents respite away from their children and a way to nurture themselves so they can care for their three kids grappling with sibling issues.

When the first weekend arrives, Glenda's parents come a day early to spend time with Glenda and Oscar. Glenda takes a few hours off in the afternoon and goes out for a walk in a nearby park with her parents and the kids. She tells her parents about her marriage and the serious injury that recently happened to Fess. She also reveals Jinx's cutting behavior and confides her feelings that Oscar puts too much pressure on Jinx to babysit Snookie because his older sister Emily did the same to him.

With relief, because she has kept all this inside, Glenda shares how the counseling for their teen daughter has pointed out that Jinx has too much responsibility at home. Glenda tells her parents how this has made her face how Emily used to push Oscar around. Suddenly, while looking up at a squirrel racing up a tree after a smaller squirrel, Glenda blurts out that her brother Chris really bossed her around, too. Glenda gets teary and her mom comforts her. Her dad, however, looks upset and walks away to tend to grandson Fess, who has climbed high on a tree.

Once her dad is out of earshot, Glenda's mother says she knows that Chris bullied Glenda even though he was younger and says she is so sorry about allowing this to happen all these years. Her mom inhales, like she is going to hold her breath, and tells her daughter that Glenda's dad had an affair when the kids were young. Although Glenda did not know this revelation, Chris did. He found out by coincidentally picking up the phone to make a call and overhearing his dad on the line with the girlfriend. Chris told his mom, then started acting out, punching and hitting Glenda and becoming, at times, belligerent. This accelerated to an even greater degree as he grew older, almost out of habit. Secretly, because they did not want the other children to know, Glenda's parents patched things up, although their marriage was never the same. Her mom says wistfully that she wishes she had enjoyed a better marriage, but she's glad she stuck in there, because she knows that the whole is more important than the parts.

Glenda's mom knew Chris, Glenda's brother, was mistreating Glenda and sees Jinx and Fess repeating the sibling pattern that Glenda and Chris acted out. Although this makes her very sad, Glenda's mom says she is so relieved that Glenda and Oscar are going away for the Marriage Encounter weekends. And while she's glad she stayed with Glenda's dad, they would have had such a better rapport and their kids would not have had such a bitter connection if she had just sought outside help like Glenda has. Fess runs up with his granddad, and Glenda looks at her happy son and feels she is so relieved her mom just shared this shocking secret for not only her own sake, but for Fess's and Jinx's security as well. Her kids are really hurting each other in the here and now, but now Glenda feels that her parents are on her side.

Gayanne and Amos Learn to Care for Themselves

Dad Amos is really stressed out over the situation in his family. He needs extra cash in the hemorrhaging economy to support his new wife, two new stepkids and one birth child. Amos's son Randy spends the weekends with him and he pays his ex-wife $1000 a month in child support. Amos badly wants his second marriage to work and his son to get along with his new stepsiblings, but things are not going well. To make this stepfamily work and these siblings get along, it will take more than intervening in each child's life to make them feel more nurtured and balanced. To succeed, Amos must also take better care of himself. So the counselor suggests that Amos start running again, something he did for years in high school to calm himself from disagreements in his own dysfunctional, struggling family. When he had fights with his older sister or his mom and his sister clashed, he ran several miles each day. He thought of this as his very own healthy drug and the endorphins created made him happier as he sped along the traffic-strangled streets. However, at this point in his life he is out of condition and his stomach has a paunch. Nevertheless, Amos thinks that running just might help him look a little better to new wife Gayanne. He decides to run every morning at 5:00 AM when he gets up to start his very long and tiring day. The counselor suggests that Amos should sometimes take Randy with him. His son is desperately in need of bonding with his dad. Amos feels this is a great suggestion and asks his birth son to join him early in the morning on the weekends when he is staying at his dad's new home.

Like Amos, you need to take care of yourself in order to better care for your children. Once you have made your list of five nurturing activities to help care for yourself, pick one activity that you could start today. For example, if you feel like you want to keep a journal about your day to day feelings, start with that. Go out and buy an old fashioned diary or create a document on your laptop or desktop computer. Diaries are essentially the ancestors of blogs, only they never get published for public review. They tell us what is happening to ourselves on a regular basis and can tell us how we feel about what is occurring. For example, if you saw the film adaptation of Maurice Sendak's beloved children's book *Where the Wild Things Are* with your daughter, because it was her favorite childhood book, you could add that as a diary entry. You might record how good it made you feel to give her this opportunity to revisit her childhood and perhaps revisit your good feelings as a young mother reading her the story. Or you might record how sad the film made her because the character Max makes your daughter (and maybe you) think of divorce and how sad that is for families going through such a trauma.

Another activity you might start is to find a fellow employee who takes a walk every day at lunchtime. Ask if you might join the person. Bring your tennis shoes to work and see if you can walk for ten to twenty minutes after you eat lunch. Maybe you work in the city and rush from the parking lot or subway to work never paying any attention to the buildings. This would give you a chance to see the surroundings for a little bit and stretch out those legs before you approach the afternoon's tasks. It also gives you an opportunity to talk with a fellow employee, maybe work on losing a few pounds and hopefully begin to store some good feelings about yourself.

Next reconnect with the friend or family member to whom you told your "I Hate You" story earlier. Use this trusted family member or friend as a support system and meet with him or her in the next few months while you undertake your self help activities. Remember our goal for you is to both manage and ultimately get rid of your negative feelings. We would like you to have an on-going buddy to share your feelings with and a partner to help you make needed change. Hopefully as you start and continue these five activities the emotions you will be sharing will be more positive, help you to feel better about yourself and your surroundings and help you prepare to tell your "I Hate You" Story to your sibling.

ঌ Chapter 4 ৵

Step Number Three: Break the Rules— Uncover Family Rules That Tell You How to Behave

Change is one of the hardest things we do. Why? Because we have a push/pull conflict in ourselves. The pull factor is moving with our clan. From Neanderthals crouching together around the fire to modern people accumulating online friends, following the herd can still mean sticking with your family. The push factor is deciding to shatter the rules that bind the clan together. Becoming an adult often means changing these family codes. But some adults make loads of old family rules their present personal set of laws. Many times this works, but occasionally these old clan codes can lead to an "I Hate You" story.

Every family has a set of laws: "Never mash spaghetti into your hair." "Do not slug your brother." "Always look out for your sister." These rules allow the family to function.

Family rules also allow kin to move forward. For example, Mom works to pay for her son's college tuition. Therefore, even if he hates it, the oldest boy must come home after school to watch the youngest. This constraint on free time saves money on day care and will help the family pay for college.

Family codes can keep chaos at bay. "Don't allow your friends to bring booze to any party at our house or there will be no more teen get-togethers." "Always get up by 7:00 AM and make your bed and lunch because I'm a single dad and have to get to work." "Every child must write his or her soccer/dance/football schedule on the kitchen whiteboard, so I know where to shuttle you after school."

Many family rules are silent. Usually no one writes them down, but they get deeply scrawled in indelible ink on our cerebrums. At times hushed codes are a deadly narrative for "I Hate You" stories.

These unspoken rules can set off grudges and excruciating pain both in the past and later in life. Ambiguous, unjust and riddled with double binds, these silent family laws can be treacherous. The brutal effects of these family credos might simmer for decades. But when we get older in years, the results can take on an incendiary life of their own. Let's look at two family vignettes with rules penned invisibly.

Some parents can pit two children against each other. Many times two boys grow up following an unspoken rule that says whoever gets the higher grade or rides his bike earlier, which can be translated to whoever accomplishes anything first, is labeled Dad's or Mom's favorite.

Remember Mike and his kid brother Daryl from chapter 1? They fiercely competed against each for their parents' approval. Their mother bragged that Mike got his first tooth and walked earlier. As a result, the boys were out to hurt each other and battled over everything from the television channel to who sat in the front seat while Dad drove to the dump. They slugged it out many a day usually until Daryl cried. As the jealous second son, Daryl was at war with Mike for half his childhood. Now that they are adults, when he learns that Mike bought a new truck, Daryl subconsciously wants to barge into the dealership and pick up a bigger and newer truck.

Let's consider another example of a harmful family rule. Families many times favor a male child over a female. In all cultures, gender dictates blindly. Parents of all societies often give more to a boy than a girl.

Earlier we discussed siblings Ginger and Bobby. Bobby always got out of doing things around the house because he was the boy. The unstated rule in their family was that girls clean and caretake and boys go to college. Bobby became a dentist, while Ginger graduated high school and became a secretary. For years Ginger wanted to be a writer, but she felt crippled by her lack of higher education. After writing down her "I Hate You" story, she began a journal and joined a writing group at a local bookstore. Although she is the caretaker for her mom, she feels secretly angry at her parents for giving more of everything to Bobby because of his gender.

Implicit family rules are silent but deadly. They can create a rasping grind between brothers and sisters, one that is hard to verbalize. As young adults, brothers and sisters may see each other on social occasions, yet grudges can make them more enemies than friends. The wall built between estranged siblings may be plastered with old slights and injuries, but the siblings may be unable to say what keeps them apart.

Rules can be heard by everyone; all we have to do is listen. Rules often start with a negative word such as *never, nowhere, no one, nothing*. Or they may begin with positive words such as *always, must, everybody*. These words signal what linguists and therapists call generalizations. When you hear a sentence that begins with one of these words, you often hear a family rule. Remember from the beginning of the chapter: "Never mash spaghetti into your hair."

There are family rules that parents say out loud. For example, "Never leave your brother alone on weekends while at your father's house. Your father is mean and that's why I divorced him." "No one in the family gets new clothes except for Judy. She's the oldest and she passes hers down to you younger girls." "Always share your doll swing with your brother, because he's the new toddler in the family."

As brothers and sisters grow up, these spoken and unspoken rules can create distance and a deadly minefield between siblings. After adult brothers and sisters form their own constellations, marry, raise their families and move away, these unhealed wounds may split open when the clan gathers again.

At midlife ritual occasions such as weddings, Easter, a baptism or a bris, adult brothers and sisters can once more feel the sharp pain of sibling rivalry that's been buried for decades.

Let's look at Ginger again. At her family reunion she and her female cousins help make all the traditional Armenian food. Eating and talking by themselves, the men in the family sit around brother Bobby's big pool. The women form a second pod on the other side, the kids splashing and diving in the middle. But when Ginger's dad admires son Bobby's brand new luxury car, yet never compliments or acknowledges the meal Ginger and the other women took hours to make, Ginger feels her heart race and her blood pressure go through the ceiling.

Mike spends $40,000 on his daughter's wedding. Daryl, still in rabid competition with his older brother, spends $60,000 on a three-day event at a five-star resort.

Both Daryl's and Ginger's minds have obsolete operating systems with rules or commands that have been there for years. Yet these rules do not organize and control the present family in any predictable, programmable way. They are antique commands that no longer work.

Daryl's old family rule tells him to never stop trying to compete with Mike. Sister Ginger's imperfect operating system tells her that boys get the biggest share and girls the leftovers. These old broken operating systems remain in our brains, substituting for the real universe in the here and now.

Today, many years later, Mike has a pot belly, high cholesterol and erectile dysfunction, while Daryl is in great shape and has an active love life with his wife. But every year Daryl shows up at the clan's yearly Fourth of July barbeque and he and Mike quarrel over who will man the grill. Daryl always sullenly concedes, and Mike gets the spatula and center stage while his younger brother drinks too much beer instead. This underscores the imperfect reality that Daryl can't ditch and the unspoken rule that says Mike is typecast as the dominant son.

The golden rule in Glenda's family, when she was growing up in the nineteen eighties, was that the boys in the family got all the attention, the biggest share of the dinner a work-weary mom made and the heftiest allowance. Her husband, Oscar, on the other hand, grew up as a Generation X'er with his single mom who worked late and depended on his oldest sister to be the enforcer. The rule in his family was you do what the older sister says or else. At eighteen, his big sister was more than happy to assume that role and ordered him around, making sure the house was clean and dinner made for their divorced and never remarried mom, who came home exhausted. The "or else" part of the rule is true even today. Even now that Oscar is remarried, has two jobs, two kids and an aching head full of worry and debt, his sister Emily continues to tell him what to do—only now it is to help care of his mom.

These parents have two different rules that they have recycled with their kids. Oscar expects his oldest daughter, Jinx, to care for the family's baby, Snookie, every day after school and on weekends.

He sees girls as the enforcers and caretakers even though he secretly really resents his sister, who is now fifty years old. He has transposed his old family rule to his new family, expecting Jinx to keep order for the family even though it is pushing her into stressed and mentally unstable behavior. Glenda, on the other hand, grew up with a tall, muscular younger brother Chris who hit her and pushed her around, even though he was a few years younger. The rule in her family was boys get to do what they want because they are better than girls. Her mom, a housewife and meek person, believed this twisted trajectory

So both Glenda and Oscar have inherited rules in their minds that were previously established in their own families' codebooks of how to run their households. The problem with this generationally repeated gender rule is that it has their oldest daughter and youngest son at each other's throats, landing Jinx in therapy with the bruises and scars on her arm signaling the serious problem of cutting.

Since this couple has decided to go to Marriage Encounter, an inexpensive way to get some help with their own relationship during all the stress with their young children, they decide to discuss these disparate rules at the weekend they will be spending with the other people at the Marriage Encounter weekend.

Glenda recalls that her parents had a silent rule that said "Always look out for your little brother." She did as they said, but felt that her parents clearly favored her brother over her. This seems to still be true today when her mom and dad live close to her brother and seem to spend more time with his kids, their other grandchildren, than they do with Glenda and Oscar's children. As Glenda and Oscar have their own sibling issues among their children with obvious jealousy and a perception of favoritism over baby Snookie,

Glenda has asked her parents for help. They have come to stay with Glenda and Oscar's three kids while the young parents go to a Marriage Encounter weekend. One of the issues Glenda plans to talk about during that weekend is the family rules she grew up with and how they have affected her own parenting and her present family rules for her own kids. She wants to fully understand her older children's jealousy of young Snookie and also wonders if she favors her son over her older daughter.

All these siblings have instilled in them corrupted, out-of-date operating systems governed by family rules that always started with words like *never, can't, won't* and *always.* This is shown in this illustration of a circle.

Ringing the circle pictured are the words *can't, won't, should, never, none* and *always.*

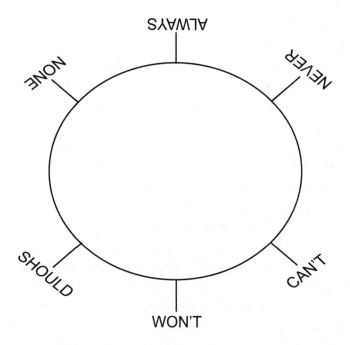

The circle is the metaphor for the parallel universe. The words clinging to the edge tell you that this person's reality cannot change. This parallel universe is an impoverished, miserable, unmodifiable world. In this pseudo reality, the sibling rival, brother Mike, remains nine years old even though he is now an overweight sixty-two-year-old with high blood pressure. But in his brother Daryl's mind, Mike is a lithe, streaking nine-year-old who wins the races Dad sets up to pit the two against each other. Daryl is stuck in a world decades old where he cannot win any races. He is stuck on a sibling past that he cannot seem to change.

In the here and now, you and your siblings may begin to come back together. You have raised your families and have more time to see your family of origin. You just may really enjoy each other's company, because your brothers and sisters, launched from the same womb, remain the people closest to you in your life. You may reunite at family reunions or share vacations, social networking or other interests like travel or genealogy.

When you see more of your brothers and sisters again as you get older, if you have a corrupted operating system with rules that don't work any longer, you are in for family trouble. Mike, who was pitted against Daryl from the first tooth they lost to swim meets, is a different guy at age sixty-two. He's lost some of his teeth, has a bridge, has sprouted a protruding belly and couldn't compete in any race no matter how much he wanted to. Daryl has the wrong image of brother Mike in his head.

In adulthood, brothers and sisters may need to change the rules they learned about their siblings in childhood, because their brothers and sisters may have changed. Their siblings may be kinder, more caring, more responsible or less selfish. On the other hand, they may be the same people they've always been.

Siblings can find themselves thrown together to help parents move, close up a family home, make hard decisions about putting

Mom or Dad in a nursing home or deal with splitting valuable family treasures like antique wardrobes and pricey paid-off houses. Brothers and sisters may struggle to distribute their parents' not-so-priceless property, valuable only in the minds of the children who grew up in that family, like Mom's chipped fairy plate collection that everyone covets.

Ritual events can throw us together with siblings and reopen the chasm that impacted us as kids. Weddings, funerals, christenings or graduations are all occasions where siblings reunite. Many times brothers and sisters are asked to take ritual roles such as godfather or bridesmaid. This can boomerang us back to the past, where a younger brother or sister was a sworn enemy. If your sibling is still your foe, what do you say to these family requests? Do you turn them down, potentially hurting the next generation, perhaps a grandson who is being christened or a daughter who is getting married?

Estranged siblings can slam into each other again in nightmare settings. An accident or marital conflict can provoke a crisis in adulthood. A sudden parental medical crisis with aging parents may land families in the emergency room. To get to this chaotic scene, brothers and sisters may have jumped on planes all over the country to gather at their father's or mother's bedside. In these moments, the ramparts supporting the sibling wall need to come down. These critical family transitions demand that siblings line up as a team. Yet here is the rub: Many times those old rules that say, "Bobby always gets out of helping Mom, so here we go again" or "Mike has always been the winner, so even if I am a physician's assistant, he'll take charge of Dad's care and push me out" sound far-fetched. Yet these types of scenarios happen all the time.

These past family rules will turn the best parent care plan into gibberish. The old codes in Daryl's and Ginger's heads are still in place, even though the operating system that classifies and controls the family is antiquated. In turn, these corrupted family rules stop change from occurring—not just for the siblings but for the ill, aging parents as well.

Find Your Old Rules

Now we would like you to search your mind, then peer between the gears governing your thoughts. We want you to see if any old rules about your adult brother or sister are lurking there. We are looking for a mental model of family rules because that's where we may find an "I Hate You" story about your sibling.

Grandmother Janet, Gayanne's mother, recalls, as she drives bickering granddaughter Vera to soccer with her angry grandson Roger in the backseat, how her own mother, Flora, told her when she was a child, the rule was always protect your sister, because family is the most important. Janet followed that rule and still has a strong relationship with her own sister, Bitsy. But the rule has since changed. Janet divorced her husband and raised her daughters, Gayanne and Bitsy, in the nineteen seventies, and the turmoil of her remarriage seemed to wedge the two sisters apart. Now Janet is driving in a car with her grandchildren, the product of her daughter Gayanne's divorce, with her grandkids being cruel to one another. The old rule of protecting one's sibling, taught by Janet's mom, seems to be erased in this new generation. Baby boomer Janet wonders how she could instill mother Flora's rule of supporting one another as siblings in her grandchildren's minds to help them avoid future "I Hate You" stories.

Dad Oscar, worried about his daughter Jinx and the bruises on her arm that he suspects are not from falling, thinks back to his own family. He focuses on the word *always*. His mother worked at an ice cream stand as the manager in a small Midwestern town where they grew up. Oscar's dad had divorced his mom in the eighties after he fell in love with another woman he dated in high school and met again at his class's ten-year reunion. After the parental breakup, Oscar was shuffled back and forth between his mom's single-parent home and his dad's house with his new stepmom, where his half-sibling and two stepsiblings lived. He really did not get along with them, but it was even tougher with his real blood sibling, Emily, back at his mom's house. "Always listen to Emily and do what she says" was his mom's iron-clad rule. The Reagan-era economic meltdown had made earnings at the ice cream shop low and his mom struggled to keep her household going, cleaning houses on the side. So Emily held the lock and key to Oscar's life in almost a reign of terror and he always had to follow what she said. If he didn't, she tattled on him and his mom grounded Oscar by taking away his new albums of Van Halen and his beloved Nirvana, whose frontman, Kurt Cobain, was the product of a miserable divorce like Oscar. When Emily told on him and his mom took away that album, it just broke Oscar's heart. He almost hated Emily. Now Oscar suspects that he might have recreated his mother's "always listen to your sister" rule with his daughter and son. He grounds Fess when he does not listen to his sister Jinx, whom he needs to watch Fess and Snookie, because he is working two jobs. But has Oscar created the same dysfunctional family rule? Will Fess grow up hating Jinx like Oscar hates his sister Emily?

Revise Your Old Rules

Now we want you to make a list of five generalizations that were used in your childhood. Get a piece of paper or your laptop. Sit in a comfortable space and rummage around in your head. See if you can retrieve five generalizations. Five is great, but a smaller number will do.

After you create your list, give some thought to how these generalizations have prevented you from changing the rules about your siblings. For example, Ginger has rarely asked Bobby to do anything to help with their elderly parents as they age because he's a boy and a dentist. So Ginger, being a girl and a simple secretary, just accepts that she should do all the work to help her parents. She has never asked Bobby to lend a hand.

When her parents decided that their house was too big for just the two of them, Ginger helped Mom and Dad go through all their possessions to decide which ones to keep, chose a realtor to sell their house, found a new house for Mom and Dad and then arranged to move everything. Bobby came over when everything was done. Ginger cannot change this generalization about her brother and it has stopped her from changing her behavior toward him all her life. She is overburdened and feels burnt out by her parents, yet she continues to follow that old family rule: "Never ask your brother to do any cleaning or caring."

Ginger is frozen in time. This archaic rule from all those years ago was created by her parents, but Ginger still abides by it faithfully. It inhabits and governs the operating system in her mind. It stops Ginger from changing and escaping the mind-set in which she carries an overwhelming family load. The word *don't* is repeating in her mind and prevents Ginger from getting into the present where she and her brother could not only trust each other, but share the care of their ill mother as well.

Generalizations and "I Hate You" Stories

Now pick two of the generalizations from your list that might reflect your own bad memories about family. Underneath your choices, jot down how these family rules may have led to your sibling "I Hate You" story.

As an example, Ginger writes down a rule about Bobby. Her rule is "Always give Bobby what he wants, because he's the boy." She continues that she recalls her mom and dad giving everything to Bobby that she never got as a kid. She goes on to say that she dreamed she could be a writer, but she was never given the chance even to go to college. She feels if she were a boy, she could have been somebody important. This is Ginger's "I Hate You" story and she lives it even today.

Family Rules You Might Be Able to Change
Now choose one of the generalizations or family rules you picked and the one you most believe you might be able to change. Daryl rereads his "I Hate You" story about Mike and writes that Mike and his wife have bought his kids expensive gifts every birthday and has never forgotten one nephew's or niece's birthday in ten years. He wonders if Mike might be a different person and, after some thought, he might change his "I Hate You" story about his brother.

Look at the generalization you chose about your sibling. We will consider productive ways you might change it in our next chapter.

Genogram of Vera, Roger and Randy's Family

To help you better understand these generational differences and how they may play a role in your "I Hate You" Story, let's explore the intra- and inter-generational connections of a modern American family. This genogram is a pictorial display of this family.

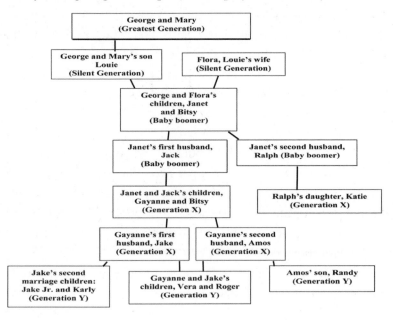

Step Number Four: Explore What Led Your Sibling to Hurt You

Every child grows up in the environment into which he or she was born. Sometimes family, society or random circumstances contribute a negative atmosphere. Max in the 2009 Spike Jones film *Where the Wild Things Are* is a good example. His parents are divorced and his mom is a single parent struggling to support Max and his fourteen-year-old sister. These circumstances create a scenario for Max to go "wild."

In the film, Max has the youngest child role in the family. His teenage sister's role is the oldest child and she plays that out cruelly as she stands by while her teenage boyfriends pummel down Max's igloo, setting the famous stage for Max to run off to where the wild things are. Role and circumstances affect our original families and can create "I Hate You" stories that last into our adulthood.

Angie's and Jennifer's Family Circumstances

Stepsisters Jennifer and Angie, whose story was told in chapter 1, were blended into a new family by some pretty harsh circumstances. Angie's mom was killed in an accident. A few years after this catastrophe, her dad remarried and his new wife became Angie's nasty stepmother. Faced with a cruel new mom, Angie believes she relived Cinderella's fate. No matter what she did, she recalls, her new stepmother ignored her, yet lavished attention on her own daughter Jennifer. Angie's dad took a nineteen fifties male approach and ignored his child's plight. Feeling trapped in a heartless clan, Angie directed her ire toward her stepsister, blaming Jennifer for Angie having a dad and stepmom she could not reproach. Angie grew up with an "I Hate You" story that festered for decades.

Ted and John's Family Circumstances
Let's look again at the circumstances of Ted and John's family (from chapter 1). Their divorced mother was frightened and ineffective. Abandoned by her husband, she was forced to go to work with few job skills. The resulting stress and desolation edged her toward a prescription drug problem. With an empty pocketbook, Ted's mom could not pay a babysitter, recruiting her older son John. Every afternoon, when the school bell rang, he had to be home to keep an eye on Ted.

Cut off from school sports, John was stuck babysitting. These circumstances fueled the teenager's resentment. One afternoon something exploded in John and he seriously injured his brother, sending Ted to the hospital with slashed feet.

Vera and Roger's Family Circumstances
Gayanne, whose kids Vera and Roger are at each other's throats, just came back from the ER, where Roger had stitches in his arm from a fight with his sister during which a glass door got between the two kids. Beside herself, she wonders where did she go wrong as a mom? But Gayanne grew up amidst some very turbulent circumstances. Her own mom, Janet, was divorced and Gayanne is a Generation X cohort from the nineteen eighties. She was raised in

an era of economic volatility when downsizing, layoffs and scarcity ruled. Mom Janet worked two jobs to get by and bought their house with a 14 percent mortgage. Gayanne felt lost at times as she listened to underground music stars Patti Smith and the Dead Kennedys. Growing up the product of divorce, she herself divorced and remarried. On top of this, son Roger is seething from having to share his room with new stepbrother Randy. So her two teenagers' potential to be future irate or seething siblings and recently ending up in the emergency room may be connected.

Glenda and Oscar's Family Circumstances

When young parents Glenda and Oscar discovered bruises on their daughter Jinx's arm that made them feel she might be cutting, Jinx was put into therapy with a counselor who specializes in teenage issues. In filling out the questionnaire for the counselor and then meeting with her, it comes out that in addition Jinx and her brother are arguing constantly and the arguments have escalated since baby Snookie was born fourteen months ago. Glenda and Oscar go over some of the circumstances they feel could have led to Jinx's issues.

Some of the current occurrences in Jinx's life are that her mom gave birth to another child, who is now a toddler. Other happenings include an economic downturn that has set red ink into the family balance sheet. The economy is tanking due to the housing bubble collapsing and the dad, Oscar, had to take a second job. The tight family pocketbook led to Jinx's horseback riding lessons being canceled to a negative balance in the family budget. Mom Glenda has worked extra hours at work to give her clan a fiscal boost. But the extra hours have meant that she exceeds the amount of time Glenda has baby Snookie in day care. So when she works past 4:00 in the afternoon, the day care van drops Snookie off at Glenda and Oscar's home. Glenda gets overtime pay and Jinx and Fess get to babysit Snookie. This has created serious fights between the two older kids. Glenda and Oscar reveal all these circumstances to Jinx's new counselor.

Family Circumstances Can Lead to Painful Sibling Events

As adults, both Angie and Ted have "I Hate You" stories. Yet neither has considered that episodes in their lives led to these toxic tales. A cracked structure of family woes can make siblings grow up in a parched world. Ted, Angie and the famous Max did not create their rickety nests. Ted and Angie teetered among the wind-blown sticks, ending up with "I Hate You" stories.

What Has Led to Your "I Hate You" Story?

What are some of the traumatic circumstances that can lead siblings to "I Hate You" stories? They include financial tempests in which parents lose jobs or homes, divorce, death of a parent, stepfamilies or any of life's tornados that turn a child's world upside down.

What we would like you to do now is think about your own family. Were there any dire events that beset your clan? When you were growing up, for example, were your parents divorced like Max's in *Where the Wild Things Are*? Did your family end up with an empty bank account or no child support, like Ted's abandoned mom? As they did for Angie, did circumstances whirl you, helpless, into a strange new family studded with snubbing stepsisters or brothers? A torrent of tragedies, caused by random events made worse by roles and rules, can beset families when kids are growing up, sometimes sinking sibling relationships.

Like storybook Max and his adolescent sister Claire, strained ties can make kids "wild" and "angry" and they sometimes wreak their revenge on a sibling. After Max's sister turns her back on him as her teenage friends wreck his fort, Max stomps into his sister's room, soaks her carpet with icy feet, then smashes the popsicle heart he gave her. Max has an "I Hate You" story.

Family Circumstances That Contributed to Your "I Hate You" Story

Now that we have seen the chaotic happenings that created Max's, Ted's and Angie's "I Hate You" stories, let's turn back to you. Can you think of a family problem that might have contributed to your "I Hate You" story? If so, make a list of outside forces that may have plagued your childhood. Please try to list at least three situations. Remember that Max's issues were divorce, low incomes wages for his mom and his sister's reaching adolescence.

Next, we would like you to write a paragraph about each family circumstance you listed and describe how that affected your feelings toward your estranged sibling. Did it make you feel embittered like Ted? The problems due to his parents' divorce left him feeling like his angry brother's victim after he landed in the emergency room. Did your family issues make you feel abandoned, like Max of the *Wild Things*? Like Angie, did your family circumstances make you feel like Cinderella? In your writings, can you show how your family circumstances and your estranged sibling in your "I Hate You" story are similar to Max's, Ted's or Angie's?

How Your Cohort Generation Affects Your Circumstances

Next we would like you to look at the cohort generation that your parents or grandparents lived through. What are the generational effects on you and your children? Remember Gayanne, a Generation X mother? Her children are really struggling right now. She's trying to blend her family with her new husband Amos's family and combine the two broods into a new version of *The Brady Bunch*. However, the merger has been besieged by problems, as the two stepbrothers despise sharing Roger's bedroom and blood siblings Vera and Roger fight continuously.

Gayanne really blames herself, but she can look back to her own cohort generation and her mother's cohort generation before that to view the family map. In that familial genogram (please refer to page 78), Gayanne might discover what historical models may have led to her present family crisis and caused her to seek a counselor.

Gayanne was raised by a mother whose nineteen sixties generation grew from the ferment of colliding values between men and women, marriage and divorce, stay-at-home moms versus working moms and the nuclear family versus the extended family.

Her mom, a baby boomer cohort, was the first woman to graduate from college in her family and the first woman to get a divorce. Although mom Janet remarried and thought she success-fully reared Gayanne, the cultural changes in her own baby boomer generation planted the seed of marital breakup for Gayanne. She married hopefully, but Gayanne's Generation X marriage dissolved as the county clerk recorded the second consecutive divorce in the family. Gayanne's cohort generation was raised by Baby Boomer mothers who imprinted the possibility of divorce and a remarriage. Right now this attempt at renewed vows and a blended family is not succeeding for Gayanne and the behavior of her two kids make her feel fed up and despondent about her family's future.

However, Gayanne can look at the past and how the evolution of marriage and family played out in succeeding generations in her kin to see what has led to this valiant attempt she is making to create a new blended family and the problems her children have encountered. Her two blood children's discord and the strained relationship between her stepson and blood children have resulted, in many ways, from the changes made by the baby boomers in how they approached marriage and family relationships. These changes were a domino effect cascading down on Gayanne's Generation X and Jinx and Fess's Generation Y, ending with Gayanne's kids in counseling.

So if you have teenagers or young children whom you feel are heading down the road to creating their own "I Hate You" stories, we would like you to think about the generational changes that occurred in your own family that might have contributed to the strife between your own children and lead to their potential "I Hate You" stories. Are you a child of Generation X, like Gayanne, who grew up with divorce? Did you yourself get divorced, and are your kids fighting among themselves like the children in Gayanne's family?

Perhaps you are a grandmother like Gayanne's mother, Janet. As baby boomers, Janet's generation led the way to gaining women's rights. But perhaps Janet needs to look back at her generation and see the effect it had on her own child Gayanne and now her grandchildren. The arguments between Vera and Roger have escalated since Gayanne's divorce and remarriage, ending with her grandson's latest trip to the emergency room. If you are a baby boomer grandmother in a similar situation with your grandchildren, reflect on how generational values, both positive and negative, have an impact on your children and grandchildren and perhaps how you would like to change them.

Generation Affect to Your "I Hate You" Story

Young parents Glenda and Oscar were very much affected by the cohort generation that their parents, the baby boomers, lived through. These generational effects cascaded onto Glenda and

Oscar as children in the nineteen eighties and have poured down on their own children Jinx, Fess and little Snookie like rain.

Oscar thinks about children Jinx and Fess arguing when they are home alone after school and recalls a picture of himself and his sister Emily battling as young kids in the eighties. When he was growing up in the Midwest, his dad left his family for another woman; Oscar's mom, meanwhile, had only a high school education and got a job at the local ice cream parlor as a manager in order to pay the bills. She worked long hours and had no money for daycare. Oscar had been in day care as a toddler, but his mom would have to pay for after-school care, so she had older daughter Emily watch Oscar after school. Emily was the enforcer in the family and the family rule was "Always listen to Emily." Oscar hated that rule, and he and Emily came to blows many times when she made him take out the trash or feed the dog after school. These are jobs in retrospect Oscar thinks were fair tasks for a young boy, but he bitterly resented being bossed around by Emily. His mom took a job with a housecleaning company as the economy got tighter and Oscar just spent more time with his sister. But he learned from the beginning that older sisters act as enforcers and he has allowed the same generational setup to occur in his own family. Daughter Jinx is the enforcer over son Fess after school, because they can't afford the extra day care for baby Snookie. So Oscar realizes that he has followed the same rule that his mom used.

His baby boomer dad is now a very conservative family man with three other adult children all around Oscar's age. When they were kids, Oscar and Emily were shuffled back and forth between his dad's new family and their own mom. At their father's place, Oscar and Emily had to contend with two new stepsiblings from their stepmother's first marriage and a half sibling, as the dad had another child with Oscar's new stepmother. Oscar never felt accepted by this new stepfamily and believed that his stepmother and dad did not go out of their way to make him and Emily feel welcomed in their new family. Oscar frequently got into arguments with his stepbrother, who was older and at times left black and blue marks on Oscar. Thinking about this, Oscar recalls the bruises on his daughter Jinx's arms.

As Oscar got older and became a teenager, the situation didn't get any better. His mom was still stuck working two jobs and older sibling Emily, who was now a legal adult at eighteen, was taking care of things at home after school. As a teen, Oscar withdrew to his favorite band, Nirvana. He idolized Kurt Cobain as a teen. When Cobain committed suicide, Oscar became very upset. He now thinks of son Fess growing up with the same rules by which he and sister Emily had to abide. Will Fess become a rebellious teen? Is Jinx's cutting a sign of serious scary things to come for her?

Oscar and Emily are reliable siblings, but Emily still bosses Oscar around. She has just asked him to start helping out with their older mom, who is showing early signs of dementia. Oscar has two jobs, three kids and a child with possible mental health issues. He does not know how he can find the time to help his mom and dreads Emily's heavy criticism, even at this point in their lives.

Roles and How They Affect Families

Now let's look at another way your family fabric can be twisted and torn, maybe leading to an "I Hate You" story. This additional path to family feuds and sibling misery is your role in the family.

In any play or drama, there are always standard roles like a leading man, a heroine, a villain and a minor character or two. Families can have central casting as well. Parents usually assign roles to family members. These roles include the oldest, who can be a bully or sometimes the child with the most responsibility. There is the classic role of the youngest, who is the baby and often the favorite. Because gender is often the elephant in the family living room, the boy can often be the most valued. The parents' favored sibling could be the oldest, the smartest, most educated or even the most physically or mentally challenged brother or sister.

Families have patterns. And trying to locate these patterns can sometimes be like navigating a map of the family genome. Roles can be a GPS to help us decipher these filial directions. The role of the youngest is seen in Max of the *Wild Things*. He morphed into a "wild thing" when his older sister stopped playing with him and joined her adolescent friends in a quest to be "popular." So role can have negative consequences, like those that beset the rejected youngest sibling Max.

In families, parents are the directors who not only create sibling roles, but also write the scripts for them. Ted's mother needed John to babysit because she had no money for day care. She looked the other way while John bossed Ted around, because without John's help she would have to quit her job, risking more misery. Angie's dad ignored the nasty abuse his new wife inflicted on his young daughter, much like Cinderella's clueless father. He chose to ignore what became a lifetime of desolation for daughter Angie.

Yet roles in families are necessary. Sometimes they act as dikes, keeping domestic torrents from sweeping away the family nest. The role of the oldest who cares for the youngest kept Ted's family barely above the high water marker. If a mom has several teenage daughters and one teen son, she might demand that the boy keep an eye out for the girls at the school dance. If a parent notes that one child is highly organized, he might have that kid take on the role of family enforcer and take charge of making all lunches or making sure the other kids do their chores.

At the same time, roles in families can sometimes actually cause injury to other siblings. Sibling Ted was sped to the hospital, where the wound caused by the anger of his brother John, had to be stitched up. Every action is an exchange and we all have the potential to cause pain to a sibling. In the film adaptation of *Where The Wild Things Are*, Max's sister Claire caused pain to Max when she stood by and let her teenage friends destroy Max's igloo, making him a "wild thing."

The Stepsibling's Role

Earlier we spoke of the dismal role of the stepsibling, ingrained in our psyche by the story of Cinderella, who was oppressed by her evil stepmother and hideous stepsisters. Divorce and remarriage produce a glut of step-relations who are often far from today's families. Stepchildren are frequently thrown together, losing half their bedrooms and battling for power and rank in a clan of children they never chose. In the original marriage, siblings had a safe home. Now they are uprooted and jammed into a new, unfamiliar house that feels far from safe. In the roles of stepsisters, Angie and Jennifer tore the sibling relationship apart for decades.

In Gayanne and Amos's twenty-first-century family, Roger, the younger sibling, and his new stepbrother Randy are both fed up and sad at having to share a room, losing their families of origin and even Roger's treasured old toys like his action figure collection. Roger had to give up his single bed for what he considers half a bed when a new set of bunk beds was installed in his room to accommodate Randy, who is only there on the weekends. Randy, on the other hand, feels like a guppy in a fish tank full of eels and sharks. He does not fit into this new abode with his dad and he fears these fellow fish will attack him and peck at his sides. He's scared, anxious and ready to burst in this new unfamiliar bedroom with Roger—his new, unfamiliar stepbrother.

The Favorite Child's Role

In some families' circumstances there is a favorite child. It could be the youngest, oldest or the kid with black hair and dimples who looks like Uncle Don. While the children are growing, they gripe, but they can do little to change things.

Tammy, whose story we related in chapter 1, was the last of five siblings. She was showered with privileges never offered to older siblings. Little Tammy paraded about in fancy new clothes from boutiques when the others had bargains from department stores. Her childhood perks included riding lessons, pricy summer camps and tuition to a respectable college. None of the brothers or sisters got such goodies. Tammy's role as the preferred child especially bruised Paula, the middle child. The unspoken law in Tammy's family was "the favorite gets the most." For decades, all the older brothers and sisters bitterly resented both Tammy and her elevated family status. The result was a fault between Tammy and her siblings, especially middle child Paula.

Tammy is getting married at thirty-five and plans a sumptuous wedding. All her nieces are asked to be flower girls, including Paula's one daughter. Tammy writes a letter to Paula to ask if her niece might be in the bridal party. Paula reads the letter, livid with anger. She sees her youngest sibling starring in another lavish event, reprising her role as favorite.

Even though Paula's six-year-old daughter would adore her gauzy white taffeta dress, the invitation infuriates Paula. Her love of her child is muffled by the memory in her mind screaming, "Tammy is the favorite!" All the generous birthday gifts her young daughter has received from Aunt Tammy can't cauterize Paula's pain. She writes back to Tammy and declines the invitation. Because Tammy's favored role in childhood hurt Paula, she still wants to hurt Tammy, even at thirty-five.

Assess the Baby's Role

If you are a parent of a young family and are reading this book, you might have a young baby in your family who is causing jealousy and bruised feelings in your other children and this just may be leading to an eventual "I Hate You" story. As your baby or toddler demands more care and security, you may have no choice but to provide a disproportionate amount of time to that child's needs. If you are now a mom or dad, you and your spouse could be working and tending to your family all at the same time, so there's a strong chance you may have to ask your oldest child to assist in the care of the baby. However, the hurt feelings on your oldest children's part should be tended to right away. You can avoid an "I Hate You" story by swabbing the bruised sibling wound right away and perhaps adjusting the care situation so it is not such a burden.

Glenda and Oscar have a fourteen-month-old baby who has been welcomed with a difficult combination of resentment and love by their two older kids. These parents both work long hours and have had to delegate care of baby Snookie to their teenagers, Jinx and Fess. Glenda works overtime and sometimes the day care sitter drops Snookie off when Glenda is still at work. When Jinx has to take over care, she is filled with the duality of love and umbrage. She is burdened with a new responsibility on top of her high school homework and trying be popular with her friends by talking and texting on her phone. Jinx has a future gripe at this babysitter role, and she may take her resentment out on Snookie years later, as Tammy's siblings have retaliated against her at thirty-five.

See the Bigger Picture

Let's return to the story of Ted from chapter 1. Remember how his brother, John, committed a sole violent act that occurred several decades ago, but left Ted feeling like a lifelong victim. He avoids his older sibling, except for isolated family gatherings. Cementing his victim role, Ted has chosen the career of a social worker, helping people in need who may be victims themselves.

Ted feels depressed, like his mom, surrounded by a veil of misery long ago. Ted is really not sure about his family's circumstances back then. He confides in a friend, a fellow social worker, and she suggests that Ted try to find out more about his parents' divorce. The social work friend recommends that Ted get in touch with his mom's aging siblings. She point out that they were contemporaries of his mother and may have some insights as to what happened when Ted was young.

Ted calls his seventy-some-year-old aunt and uncle and offers to take them out to dinner. Struggling to say what he means, he asks what led to his mom and dad getting divorced. Ted finds out that his dad moved to Northern California after World War II and never returned. His aunt recalls Ted crying when he was in third grade because classmates made fun of him "not having a daddy." His aunt adds angrily that the boys' father just stopped sending any money to his estranged family. Without any real job skills, in an era when few women went to college or worked, Ted's mom, according to her brother, got a job in at a local department store. Ted also discovers that his mom lapsed into clinical depression and was prescribed an antidepressant. His aunt reluctantly tells her nephew his mom overused the medication, making her feel "out of it" at times.

Ted's uncle tells him thirteen-year-old John was a star athlete in his junior high and had to give up sports to babysit Ted.

What Ted has been able to see from these talks with family is the larger picture that describes the circumstances that led young John to detonate and cause Ted to be rushed to the hospital for stitches.

Finding Your Own Big Picture
Grandmother Janet knows the bigger picture in her family and is thinking of sharing it with her daughter, Gayanne. She recalls

growing up with the solid values of her Depression era parents, Flora and Louie, who held their family together with Louie's strong work ethic and family-centric values where the family takes care of itself and siblings are always loyal to each other because the family's economic survival is at stake. Janet can see where she herself veered off in the late nineteen sixties. She divorced and now her daughter Gayanne, a Generation X child, has followed suit. The circumstances Janet lived through include the Vietnam War, the volatile, loud beginning of the women's movement and the upheaval of the Civil Rights era. Janet's mother Flora's Depression era values were smashed by Janet's sixties circumstances and values.

But Janet knows that deep in the core of her family, her parents' family values remain. Janet has always been loyal to her children and has that deep core of family-centric values. She knows she needs to be there for her daughter through these turbulent times with Janet's grandchildren. Perhaps she can sit down with Gayanne and pass on some family history and the bigger family picture along with the assurance that they come from a family that is always there for each other. Janet will be the bulwark to support Gayanne and drive her grandchildren wherever they need to go to help keep Gayanne's blended family together.

Finding Your Family's Big Picture

If you can't recall or never were aware of key circumstances in your family, we would like you to ask a member of your family who was around when you were growing up what those family circumstances were. It may take a phone call and a visit or dinner date like Ted made with his aunt and uncle. Exploring this background will help you to find out about family roles in your youth. After you talk to family members, jot down what you have learned. Describe the family circumstance that you did not know before.

Unfair rules or dire circumstances, like parents losing their jobs, divorce or the death of a parent or a sibling can lead to an "I Hate You" story. Understanding the bigger picture means tracking down family history and filling in the blanks.

A Sibling Who Hurt Us in the Past May Not Hurt Us in the Present

Let's fast-forward to the present. John and Ted have grown up and John is not likely to injure Ted again. In fact, if Ted brought up this past story of the slit feet, John just might say he's sorry. When Max grows up, he might tell Claire how angry it made him when she let her friends destroy his igloo. Claire might say she loves Max and is sorry she hurt him. She was just trying to be popular. Angie and Jennifer are now adults with kids of their own. Angie tells her "I Hate You" story repeatedly and her teenage daughters wish she would get over it. They love Aunt Jennifer, have fun with their cousins and really don't want to listen to Mom's old tales. Yet Ted's, Max's and Angie's stories are incidents that resulted in hurts that really happened.

Tammy is in her thirties and now far from a baby. She may be a really nice, caring person. In fact, she's been sending cards and gifts to all her nieces and nephews for years. Tammy even tried to get to know estranged sister Paula better. Recalling that Paula loved expensive nightgowns, Tammy went to her own favorite San Francisco store and picked out a very expensive penoir set for Paula, mailing it off and saying that she really wanted to get to know her better and be friends.

How Roles Played Out in Your Family Drama

Now let us revisit your "I Hate You" story. Can you see how your role or your sibling's role might have figured in the creation of this "I Hate You" story? Can you recall how your family circumstances might have played a part in that pain-filled narrative? Consider what you learned from friends or family when you gathered for your larger family's bigger picture.

We would like you try to write down what you think led to your "I Hate You" story, paying attention to roles, rules and circumstances. Make a list of all the family rules that you felt contributed to your "I Hate You" story. Create a list of all the circumstances that may have helped create your childhood wounds. Catalog the "big picture" historical details that you feel contributed to your sibling narrative.

Next write a few paragraphs describing how rules, circumstances and unearthed family history were threads in the creation of your "I Hate You" story. Perhaps you will revise your "I Hate You" story. Once you have taken these steps, we would like you to contact your trusted friend and read what you have written. If you have revised your sibling tale, discuss it with your friend. Get his or her opinion of what happened and describe how you are progressing with your therapeutic activities. Then you will be ready to take the next step.

Chapter 6

Step Number Five: Uncover How Your Sibling Still Wounds You

The past can be a prison that stops us from changing. The bars are yesterday's rules, roles and circumstances. We create our own cells and sometimes our cellmates. Those fellow prisoners can be brothers, sisters or family members padlocked with us through our "I Hate You" story. Those stories are memoirs of what happened long ago. By replaying them over and over in our minds, we lock ourselves in the past. The keys to our cell doors are moving into the present.

Look back at stepsister Angie's story in our earlier chapters. She is fixated on her "I Hate You" story. Yet in the present, Angie's daughters want to be friends with their cousins, stepsister Jennifer's kids. But the young people are roadblocked by their mom's ancient fight with her stepsister. Angie's daughters really love their Aunt Jennifer and her kids and were not even born when this stepfamily began. Yet a generation later, all family members are impounded in Angie's cell of memory. The "I Hate You" story has imprisoned this clan in all of the stepsibling memories they hate.

How Family Members Are Imprisoned in Past Roles and Family Rules

Family rules are the cold concrete of our cell walls, confining us in the past. Let's look back to chapter 1. Remember the story of siblings

Ginger and Bobby, who observe a paralyzing rule created by their parents, passed on for generations, proclaiming their clan favors a male child over a female.

Finding Your Own Big Picture

This ossified gender-based rule led Ginger to become a secretary while Bobby went to dental school. Decades later the two siblings need to care for their aging mom. Yet this old edict still locks them in the past. Bobby does nothing to help out his mom, whether its making lunches, giving her medication or doing the dishes. He says he's too busy because he's an important professional. Ginger, meanwhile, is still angry that her parents never sent her to college, yet she treats her mom with kindness. Even though her mom always has a smile for Bobby and work for Ginger, Ginger is a devoted caretaker, in spite of the past. She's mad that her brother never lifts a finger, yet she never confronts him because Bobby's the boy and his gender trumps her viewpoints. Ginger is the one who bears the pain through low self-esteem and high blood pressure. Wounded by her sibling's selfishness and parents' ancient law, her solution is to suffer. About the only thing Bobby has done is join an Alzheimer's support group because colleagues from his dental society suggested this. *Big deal*, Ginger thinks, *He's only helping himself.* This brother and sister are locked in a penitentiary of the past by the steel bars of their family's own bad rulebook.

Gayanne, Amos, Roger, Vera and Randy's Family Rules

Let's look again at a younger family—Gayanne and Amos and their kids Roger, Vera and new stepbrother Randy. Gayanne grew up in a baby boomer family where her parents, Janet and Jack, got divorced when Gayanne was eight. Baby boomer Janet remarried once but divorced again after a few years. Gayanne's family rules say remarriage does not work out. Yet she has fallen in love again and desperately wants her new marriage to be successful. Gayanne's mom, Janet, had a stepchild when she briefly remarried. The girl, a teenager, was so bruised by Janet and her dad's remarriage that she despised her new stepmother Janet and barely talked to Gayanne and her sister Bitsy.

With this stigma hanging over her new nuptials, remarried mom Janet did not know she should seek help to blend her two families together. It was in the early eighties back when there was not yet a template available to integrate stepchildren. Everyone who had seen *The Brady Bunch* in their youth thought you just tied the knot, got the TV maid, Alice, and the rest rolled out like a perfect pie crust. There was certainly no rule that said you seek a third-party counselor to help guide you through the process to make all new stepchildren adjust to each other and the stepparents.

So Gayanne has an unworkable family rule that says stepchildren don't like each other and if you marry again after divorce and have stepchildren, it will not work out. Trying to break that rule, Gayanne has instituted counseling as a way to blend her two children and new husband Amos's son, Randy. She needs the therapy, because the boys already have to share a room and all three step- siblings are acting out and miserable.

Gayanne's counselor has a suggestion for both testing and changing this twisted family rule. To help Gayanne and Amos make their union more successful, she recommends marriage counseling for them. At first, they both reject the idea saying that they just got married and marriage counseling sounds threatening. The therapist they work with says many couples do marriage counseling before marriages and all through a marriage. Since marriage these days has a less than 50 percent chance of working, she says it is an insurance policy. She warns that they certainly have a red flag cautioning them that they are in trouble, given the case of Roger's recent serious injury. If Amos and Gayanne cannot succeed as the caretakers in keeping their marriage together, how will they be able to help struggling siblings Vera and Roger get along? Furthermore, how will they be able to join stepsiblings Randy, Vera and Roger into one united family? Reluctant, Gayanne and Amos decide they will start marriage counseling. The therapist arranges an inexpensive counselor through the local family services agency that will take payment on a sliding scale, and they unenthusiastically agree.

The second suggestion that the counselor makes is that they have a family meeting with stepsiblings Randy, Roger and Vera, suggesting the two parents work out many issues by using a technique called a "Go Around". The therapist explains that they will hopefully be able to get each sibling to talk about what is good in their new blended family and what is difficult, which could bring up the strife between the siblings. This would allow the stepsiblings to talk openly in a setting where they would have a parent-mediator who could help everyone in this struggling step-clan discuss and resolve their problems.

Gayanne and Amos are told by their therapist that a family meeting would allow them to have all three children talk about what each perceives is bad about the family atmosphere through the utilization of this "Go Around" technique. This way each child can make a choice to open up and say what he or she feels without the parents forcing an encounter in the already fractious group. These siblings entered the second marriage without their own choice or consent. They have really been forced together as stepsiblings by their parents' new love and marriage. They need a voice in what is going on to solve these internal family conflicts, says the therapist. Vera may be able to talk about her anger toward her brother Roger, which has graphically come out in memories of the sliced arm Roger got when they fought over opening the glass door between them. Roger could possibly express not so hidden antagonism toward his sister now morbidly illustrated by the ten stitches he has in his arm, held temporarily in a sling. Randy may be able to express his sad and angry feelings that he has been dumped into a family with two stepsiblings and losing his dad a second time to a new stepmother.

The therapist also advises Gayanne and Amos to utilize the family meeting to set new rules for the family and siblings. One rule that is obviously needed is no fighting or hitting. Another rule can be to "use your words and talk about your feelings rather than lock doors and hit." There will be consequences for not following the rules these two parents set in the family meeting. One consequence of any hitting or shoving will be that the kids' cell phones will be taken away if they physically attack a sibling. This poses a problem since Amos and his ex-wife have to get their rules and consequences in line. However, the rule now is any kid who physically punches or pushes another will lose his or her phone for two weeks.

Stepbrother Randy has been deeply affected by his parents' divorce. He is a gifted child who really loves school and loses himself in the classroom, where he gets lots of attention from his positive interactions with the teacher. This fills in for the interest he is lacking from his dad. Randy needs a place to study on the weekends and sharing a room with Roger does not lend itself to his reading quietly alone. Roger blasts teeny bopper music, which Vera thinks is lame. But Roger still likes it and blasts the music while Randy tries to study. In the family meeting the therapist suggests discussing rules for quiet time, most notably sharing space, which all three siblings find annoying and feel angry about. The new rules which the parents express must be explained and discussed with the kids. Doing this together, suggests the therapist, could be a bonding experience for the stepsiblings even though gaining consensus could be difficult, but it is all part of learning to live together.

The counselor also proposes Amos talk to his ex-wife about agreeing to give special attention and activities for son Randy. Randy and Roger are unhappy stepsiblings because they are sharing a room. But Randy has two blood parents who can help him and the counselor encourages Amos to work together with his ex-wife on outlets for Randy that can fill in the void created by his parents' divorce. A meeting is arranged between Amos and his ex over at her new house and Randy's home during the weekdays. Since Randy really excels in school and has tested in the gifted range, he was put into the gifted and talented program in his school. The ex-spouses meet after school when Randy's mom usually picks him up after work. She occasionally has to work overtime since her employer has fired several of her co-workers. She tells Amos she's happy just to keep a job in a bad economy, so when she works over-time, she needs him to pick up Randy. Amos is really overwhelmed already with his multiple jobs and kids. However, he asks if it is okay to have Janet, Gayanne's mom, pick Randy up in these emer-gencies. Amos's ex-wife feels this is wrong and demands that Amos do the pickups, not Janet. Amos's ex's mom lives three hours away or she herself could get Randy, and Amos's mother has early Alzheimer's. This roadblock is solved by Amos and his ex-wife voluntarily going back to the marriage and family therapist who did mediation in their divorce several years before. The ex-wife relents and Janet, the stepgrandmother, is allowed to pick Randy up when he stays after school to attend the gifted and talented activities class. This gives them a chance to bond as well.

Let's return to the young family of Glenda and Oscar, who have seen favoritism issues because of baby Snookie and male child Fess.

They have come to this realization through a family crisis when they discovered that teenager Jinx is possibly cutting. The counselor they turned to suggested the way they are parenting their children may be a setup for feelings of favoritism over baby Snookie and gender bias and favoritism toward son Fess amongst the siblings. The therapist has warned them that future "I Hate You" stories could evolve among them and that Jinx's cutting may be a signpost that warns the couple to give serious thought about changing their style of parenting.

Oscar's birth family favored his sister Emily, who was the enforcer in place of her mother at home and kept her little brother in line, Oscar now worries that son Fess, who is almost a teen, will grow up with the same rules he and sister Emily had. But since he and his wife Glenda grew up with conflicting family rules about which gender was favored, they feel that they have a mess on their hands and they know it because of Jinx's self-mutilating activities.

Another suggestion the counselor has for these parents and children is to have a family meeting. This one will consist of Glenda, Oscar and their kids. Jinx may be partly reacting to her mom's favoritism of Fess, a pattern Glenda and Oscar learned in their own families of origin, the results of favoritism between boys and girls. Jinx, who, as we discussed earlier, is in individual counseling, complains to her mom and dad all the time about this favoritism toward Fess. In addition she is made to be the enforcer and the diaper changer.

Thus, the counselor recommends, as in the earlier case study, having a family meeting with the "Go Around" technique about what is good and bad in the family and how these dualities may bring out such complaints over gender and equality. The tool of the family meeting may give this mom and dad a chance to hear both Fess's and Jinx's points of view in a safe, mediated environment and get these feelings of family discrimination out in the open so they as parents and as a family can change the rules and Glenda and Oscar can change their parenting style. A second topic in the family meeting will be the older two kids' collective complaint that baby Snookie is now the family favorite and also a burden to them because they have to watch her after school when Glenda and Oscar work late.

Circumstances in the "Here and Now" That Are Hurtful
In chapters 4 and 5, we suggested you write what led to your "I Hate You" story, paying attention to roles, rules and circumstances. You followed up by getting in touch with your trusted friend and sharing this new version of your story. Now we would like you to identify something your sibling may be doing in the present that's a repeat of your past discord. Let's look at what angry siblings from previous chapters say is still repeated in the here and now.

Ted catalogs everything his brother John is doing now that continues to hurt him. He complains that John still takes over every family gathering by being a loudmouth and dominating the family conversation. This not only has Ted fuming but also he says the sound of John's grating voice makes his heart hammer like a helpless victim.

Paula's primary complaint involves her youngest sibling's upcoming wedding. Paula is riled, because Tammy is again the star of the family with her over-the-top extravaganza. In Paula's mind, everyone is pandering to Tammy once more, making her the center of attention. Paula feels this is a repeat of the old song and dance from their childhood. Tammy's renewed star power makes Paula feel inconsolably miserable and perennially second best.

Daryl is in his fifties, but he still has the same problems with his brother Mike. Every major holiday, Daryl carps while Mike takes over the important jobs like manning the barbeque or playing Santa at the family Christmas party. Daryl believes Mike still wins all the time and it's inconceivable to him that he could ever beat his older brother. Even in midlife, Daryl winces, Mike remains the favorite son.

Angie tells us that Jennifer still plays that role of the mean stepsister. At the top of Angie's list is the protest that Jennifer still gets everything and everyone still sees her as the good-looking daughter. Angie says she still suffers as the ugly stepsister—unloved and full of pain.

Glenda and Oscar decide to have a family meeting at the suggestion of their counselor and encourage siblings Jinx and Fess to talk about what is happening right now between themselves and their little sister Snookie. These parents want to use the family meeting to find out what each sibling thinks is a problem and make a plan to fix it. The therapist tells them this will help get the sibling problems out in the open and that the parents can make a list of what is frustrating the older kids about Snookie.

As a teen, Jinx thinks this is a lame idea, but her parents say this is non-negotiable and they sweeten the deal by ordering take-out from Jinx's favorite fast food restaurant as a treat. It is Girl Scout season, and they give Jinx the money to buy several boxes of the organization's most popular cookie from neighbors. Fess goes along with it, because he loves the fast-food place's French fries.

The two kids get a chance to talk about their grievances involving their baby. Jinx says that the first problem is that she has to watch Snookie after school when she has homework to do and is already having problems in her classes. Second she says that she ends up changing all of Snookie's diapers and Fess is never asked to do the dirty work. Fess, on the other hand, is really angry, because Snookie has no rules by which she follows. She is allowed to come in his room and knock down his model buildings, and he ends up having to clean up the mess as she can't do it. He also says that he feels like he's forced into being an adult when he is ten because Snookie is the new baby and he used to be.

Why Your Sibling Still Hurts You

Now, we would like you to make a list of what your brother or sister still does that really makes you angry and hurt—not in the past, but right now, at this very moment. This can be a list several sentences or many pages long, whatever format you need to fully describe your sibling problem. After you have finished, we would like you to call your trusted friend again and make a date to get together. When you meet, tell or simply read what you wrote about your sibling's abrasive behavior.

In the meantime, continue to be kind to yourself. Nurture your mind and body with the same activities you chose in chapter 3. Make yoga, mediation, mindfulness or positive activities you are doing part of your everyday schedule. Practice remaining in the moment while you're at the grocery store, driving or doing any routine task. Be present for your kids by looking in their eyes as they talk. Reconnecting with your sibling is very hard, painful work, and we want you to make sure you are treating yourself with kindness.

Gayanne makes a list of what her kids Vera and Roger are now doing to hurt each other in the present. They are constantly quarrelling, they defriended each other online, and they just got into a shoving match near a French door that resulted in a sutured arm and Gayanne increasing her counseling visits. Randy hates Roger blasting teen pop when he listens to rock and he would love a quiet period, as he is an A student and needs to study on weekends. Randy feels that he has no place to study in their cramped room on weekends, and it drives him crazy that Roger has more space than he does, as it is all Roger's space in the first place since it is Roger's old room. Step-sister Vera is full of drama and teenage angst and wears black clothes, and Randy feels he has enough drama because of his parents' divorce and his dad's remarriage, so he doesn't like living with Vera. He feels like he is in one of the old John Hughes movies he loves to watch — only his life is real.

Helping Children's Relationships

The marriage and family therapist has recommended that to help their kids Gayanne and Amos both need to start caring for themselves. Gayanne has heard of a mindfulness class for stress reduction that is being taught through her medical group. She has agreed to sign up for an eight-week class that starts that week with a book by John Cabot Zinn and learning breathing exercises to relax. Amos works two jobs and tells the counselor he has no idea how he will fit another thing in. The counselor asks what he is doing to help both stepbrothers get along. Amos says he is taking Randy to Little League and has considered being an assistant to the coach. The counselor asks if the activity he chooses could be taking both boys to their Little League games. Amos looks overwhelmed but he understands that to heal the problem between the boys and the split bedroom, he himself has to step up to the plate and interact with the two boys. He loved Little League as a kid and feels this would be a great activity for him, so he commits to driving both boys to their practices, attending everyone's games and becoming the assistant coach of Roger's team.

Vera, Roger and Randy's Hurts

The couple's therapist suggests that this family, like earlier ones, have a family meeting to discuss the stepsiblings' strife in their family. In the "Go Around" technique that they use anger and frustration is expressed by all participants. Vera feels so upset she is barely be able to sit still in the meeting. Roger and Randy are able to express their misery over sharing a room from different points of view. Randy has no place to study, Roger wants to blast his own music without stepbrother Randy whining about it.

A few solutions are proposed by dad Amos after hearing what he already knew to be a giant threat to this stepfamily's potential for harmony. He says there is a hallway alcove in the house that he can ask Gayanne's dad, Jack, to help him retrofit. It is on a quiet side of the house near the laundry room and Amos feels that this would give his son Randy some privacy to study on weekends. Grandpa Jack still is filled with remorse about his long-ago divorce from ex-wife Janet. They are getting along better as they start to work together to help their daughter. He agrees to construct the built-in desk and add a sliding door so Randy can have a small study space made out of the unused alcove. But Jack, wanting to resolve the situation he caused, goes further and volunteers to take Randy to the library on weekends occasionally. Baby boomer Jack was a scholarship student who spent many years in a carrel in his library studying hard while his fellow students were out on the streets protesting. One of the big rifts between him and Janet was that he was a conservative child of the sixties who wore short hair, worked a steady job and wanted a wife who was a stay-at-home mother. Above all else, he loves his grandchildren Vera and Roger and really wants to show his love for his new stepgrandson Randy. Janet is helping Roger by taking him after school, making a baby book and keeping Roger's drums at her house. Jack decides he will pitch in to help daughter Gayanne and her kids by offering to support stepgrandson Randy.

Stepbrother Randy also complains at the family meeting that he has no pets anymore. When his parents divorced, they both moved.

His mom relocated to an apartment that did not accept pets, so she gave Randy's beloved dog to an animal shelter, where it was adopted. This has devastated Randy. His dad Amos hears this problem in the "Go Around" at the family meeting. He knows he should have found a way to keep the dog, Boots, but comes up with an idea that Randy likes. The local American Society for the Prevention of Cruelty to Animals has a Doggie Day Care service to raise extra money to care for all the animals that are in the shelter. Amos asks Randy if he would like to volunteer at Doggie Day Care to walk the dogs. Amos has spoken to his ex-wife and she agrees that Randy can volunteer there. Grandpa Jack again offers to drive Randy to and from his volunteering at the ASPCA once a week. This is an excellent solution worked out through this struggling step-family bringing up their problems at the family meeting.

Vera is also having a hard time in school. Gayanne has already gone to her guidance counselor and asked for tutoring. It turns out the school has a free after-school tutoring class. Vera hears this with the lament that is this a modern day version of the teenage film favorite from the nineteen eighties *The Breakfast Club*, but her mom insists it is not. At the family meeting the parents emphasize that studying is important to all their kids and they set quiet times in all bedrooms. This applies on Mondays through Thursdays when Randy is not there but at his birth mother's.

In the family meeting both Gayanne and Amos go over the family rules that all three children will have to follow. Randy needs quiet to study and both Vera and Roger need to keep music and noise to a low pitch when he is around. The rule that there is no hitting or shoving, which just caused a major injury to Roger, is reviewed. The parents want to encourage more communication techniques among these stepsiblings at the family meeting as a way to get more interaction. They can be there to help the three youngsters express their feelings and hope that this will eventually lead to more communication among the three children.

Traits Your Sibling Had As a Kid and Still Has
Now we would like you to look at your own family traits. What we have been doing throughout this book is observing family behavior. Personality traits are part of individual behavior. Many traits remain with us all our lives, but some go away, especially as we reach midlife. We've looked several times at the story of Max in *Where the Wild Things Are*, because it reveals certain nine-year-old traits. He was rebellious, immature, ill-behaved and blamed others for everything. Circumstances like divorce and his sister choosing her peers rather than her little brother colored his behavior. But we can imagine as Max grew to an adult many of these traits transformed. This happens to most of us. Personality traits disappear and at times reappear. Two siblings constitute the longest human relationship, and they both have the ability to change. So, like Max and his sister, your adult sibling's personality traits may have altered.

Let's look at the siblings discussed earlier to see which personality traits have stayed the same and which ones have vanished.

We'll start with Bobby, Ginger's brother. When he and Ginger were growing up, Bobby had a egotistical personality. He studied hard from first grade on. Bobby was always in the top "Blue Bird" reading group, then in accelerated classes with his fellow nerds. He was high achieving and always thought he was smarter than everyone else. Ginger's parents never expected their male child to help with anything, so Bobby skipped chores around the house. Inconsiderate, he never plugged in a vacuum cleaner and never pitched in as Ginger did all the housework. He was the first family member to graduate from college. More educated than Ginger, he always reminded her of his superiority.

Bobby's egotistical personality has continued into adulthood. He still believes he is more intelligent and successful than his sibling. As a result Bobby remains inconsiderate and unwilling to help, never offering to assist Ginger with the care of their mother, who is suffering from cognitive impairment. He acts as though, compared to him, Ginger is dumb and unimportant.

One trait has led to the possibility of modifying the connection between the two siblings. Bobby still listens to his peer group. He has complained to fellow members at the local dental association about his mother's confusion and increased needs. Many have older moms of their own and suggest that Bobby get involved with an online support group sponsored by the Alzheimer's Association. They tell him he can better cope with his mom plus gain a professional edge with the increased number of older patients who may come his way.

Let's turn to Jennifer, Angie's stepsister. When their families merged, Jennifer, a child of divorce, did not trust anyone. Jennifer was uncertain of her new blended family, so she totally resisted getting to know Angie. During much of their childhood, she was jealous and surly to her new stepsister. No matter what her mom and new stepdad did, Jennifer hated the whole idea of being the Brady Brunch. In fact she now admits she was really afraid to share her mom with Angie. Secretly, she fervently hoped that her mother and biological dad would reconcile. Divorce was excruciating and she took her heartbreak and rage out on Angie.

Jennifer's mom and new stepdad never went to counseling to try and figure out how to merge their two families. They had no strategies or tools to help them stepparent. They never talked about the conflict between Jennifer and Angie, leaving it a major problem. The rules in the new stepfamily were inconsistent and made no sense. In fact, Jennifer's old family rule was that children do not do chores and that continued to apply to Jennifer. The rule in Angie's original family was that kids always do most of the everyday jobs around the house. Angie's dad made Angie live her first family's rule in their second family. So Angie did the housework and Jennifer did her nails, because there were no new or consistent rules in the blended family—just the old rules from each pre-divorce family. Jennifer was, in fact, gone every weekend to see her dad. Since most of the chores happened on Saturday and Sunday, they landed in Angie's lap. Jennifer did not feel secure or loved in this new stepfamily. Her mother felt very guilty about the terrible toll divorce took on her daughter. To compensate and make herself feel less blameworthy, she asked very little of Jennifer.

But a lot has happened to Jennifer since she grew up. She's been married and divorced and has stepchildren of her own. Her new marriage is very secure. So she has learned how to trust and how to be loved. She's no longer that hurt, angry person. Before they got married, she and her second husband went to counseling to figure out how to blend their families. The counselor taught her how to set rules for all the children from both marriages. She wants the stepsiblings to have the consistent rules and love she feels she missed. She has created new family rituals to help them be a unified family. Jennifer's counseling has taught her a lot about what happened to her and Angie as kids. This led her to encourage her stepdaughter and daughter to be friends with Angie's daughters, plus embrace them herself. Jennifer has many personality traits that have changed for the positive.

Finally, let's take a look at Mike and Daryl's sibling problems. As a kid Mike wanted to improve himself physically and played every sport. He had a confident smile and got along with all his friends and teammates.

As an adult, Mike is still a good buddy. In fact he always tried to be pals with Daryl, even though they were pitted against each other as kids. Mike's self-improvement has defaulted to reading and travel. A former star athlete, he is now overweight and flabby, and his sports equipment is unused.

He's still the favorite in the family and makes sure he plays the role of the chief cook at the yearly family barbeque. However, Mike has become a thoughtful guy. Instead of being self-indulgent, he's now generous. He and his wife never forget any of their nephews' and nieces' birthdays and always buy gifts for the members of the family, including Daryl's sons. Like Jennifer, Mike has made some positive changes in his own right.

Choose One Sibling Trait That Has Changed
Make a list of all the traits the sibling in your "I Hate You" story had when you were growing up. Then list all the personality traits he or she has today. Have any of those childhood traits disappeared? Add them to your list. After you have done this, call your trusted friend, make time to get together and, at the meeting, discuss whether your sibling is the same person as the one described in your "I Hate You" story and talk about his or her present actions and traits. This can convey how he or she might be a surprising new person.

Chapter 7

Step Number Six: Find Ways You Can Make Yourself Happy and Value Your Sibling

Change is one of the steepest slopes we climb. It means going against lifelong patterns. You have already shown an appetite for change and stopped reliving the bad moments of your old sibling relationship. You began a conversation with yourself about how you were hurt in the past and have measured how your sibling has altered or stayed the same in the present. Now we are going to look at another possible transformation. We would like you to consider how you yourself may have changed.

To switch to a better mind-set where you can heal, we previously suggested that you become your own caregiver and start therapeutic activities. Now that you have begun walking that new mountain road, we would like you to chart your current success. Before you approach your sister or brother and tell him or her your "I Hate You" story, you need to measure your own positive feelings.

Therapeutic Activities to Prepare You to Contact Your Estranged Sibling

Our ultimate goal is to end your suffering on the journey of your life. Instead of scowling at a digital picture of yourself and pushing the delete button, we want you to look at your image on the way up the incline and say, "What a great photo of my achievement!" With these new upbeat feelings you will find the courage to tell your "I Hate You" story to your brother or sister. In order to have that self-confidence about yourself in your present life, you must dedicate some time to your own reconditioning. Massage, exercise, journaling and meditation were some healthy choices you might have made to support your own renewal. We asked you to pick at least one activity, then start it within a week. Hopefully you are developing a fitter lifestyle through walking, yoga or a good personal choice that helps you feel physically stronger and more emotionally centered. The end result should have been less anger, anxiety and stress. This new attunement to your well-being should help you mindfully approach and talk with your sibling.

How Other Siblings Change Themselves Before Telling Their "I Hate You" Stories

Let's consider the progress of siblings whose stories we discussed in previous chapters.

Ted's transformation shows how he's caring for himself. He's dedicated time and energy to his health by joining a gym. After some historical sleuthing, he sees the big picture of his family's past. But when his sibling wound isn't cauterized by his own private efforts, he seeks counseling. The marriage and family therapist Ted chooses tells him he still is "stuck" in his rage and resentment over what happened with his brother long ago. Seeing him once a week, the therapist attempts to break up the emotional scar tissue. She helps him better understand how his immature, ill-prepared mother put too much pressure on his older brother, resulting in John's emotional explosion. Ted begins to accept the universal view of his family history. Yet, even with this fuller family portrait, Ted's mind harbors memories that leave him stalled in the past and unable to tell his "I Hate You" story to John.

The counselor suggests a meditation class. Joining a local group, Ted begins to pay attention to his own feelings in the moment and how his deep-seated fears keep dragging him back into his childhood. The breathing exercises he learns in the class slowly help Ted to break up his inner logjam. In the beginning of the sessions, Ted concentrates on observing the present, but his mind brings him back to his youth. After meditating for a few months, his mind starts to calm. Ted has gained greater clarity on how to spend more time in the present, not looping back to the deep-seated fears of a dysfunctional childhood.

In counseling, he is also moved to see how he trapped his own sons in his old sibling pattern. Ted admits to the therapist that he and his wife sometimes favor their oldest boy. By modeling the ruinous relationship he had with his older brother, the therapist warns Ted, he may pass on his harmful past to the next generation. She suggests that Ted might consider changing his parenting style with his young sons. Ted begins to spend more time with both boys, consciously giving them equal attention. Seeing there were times when it was convenient for his oldest son to babysit for his youngest, he recognized the pattern repeated from his family of origin. Conscious of how he dragged the past into his present, Ted and his wife start to make sure the only child care they arrange is an outside babysitter and vow to never shackle the youngest boy to the oldest. As Ted's present gradually becomes unstuck, he moves to change himself and his family. Mindfully awakened to new choices, he has begun to take a step toward approaching his brother to tell his "I Hate You" story.

Ginger Gears Up to Change

Instead of the automatic transmission that drives you through life, focusing on your health puts your hands on the stick to shift up to a higher gear.

Hindered by her own past pain, Ginger has decided she needs to propel herself toward an improved quality of life. Journaling for a month, Ginger sees her state of being as overwhelmed. By reading her entries each week she realizes that, like a wounded animal, she is trapped in the daily care of her mother. Since brother Bobby has touted his support group online, she decides she might follow him by signing up for a local group that convenes at a nearby community center. Feeling isolated and dumped-upon, she wakes up to her needs to get out more and work on her self-esteem. Since Bobby won't help, she hires a care provider from a local senior agency, who comes regularly to her mom's, makes dinner, leaves lunch and gets her mother ready for bed. Her shoulders feel lighter after each meeting of the support group she has joined and having evenings to herself. Ginger has begun to treat herself with a new sense of tenderness.

What Makes Siblings So Important?

Even if they have an "I Hate You" story, many siblings believe that their brothers or sisters are important enough to try to get to the bottom of these angry or sad feelings. Siblings mean so much, because they share a sameness that can give us a feeling of comfort. If we are blood siblings, we come from the same gene pool. This sometimes gives us an inner feeling of unity. This common DNA can symbolize the naturalness and rightness of genetic bonds. That's why genealogy is so important to some of us.

Siblings can share class, race or the same cultural heritage. You can brag that your family is from the same upper class that knows what to do with all the silverware next to the plates when you sit down for a formal meal. Or you can be proud that you and your siblings share the same racial background. Perhaps you can say your family is from the same geographical region of the world. For instance, you are all Italian so your family makes the best pasta dish, or your family is Japanese so you all honor elders.

Culture can mean your family did things in a certain way or in a certain order. Perhaps one side of your family opens gifts on Christmas Day, while the other side opens their presents on Christmas Eve. Or you can brag that in your family, your mother made cakes only from scratch. These family cultures make a difference when a person marries into another family, forcing siblings to blend together. The result can be a clash of cultures, especially if one family has certain traditions on Christmas Eve while the other has similar traditions on Christmas Day.

Beyond cultural heritage, siblings can share the same secret language and common memory. Brothers and sisters have a personal knowledge that only siblings who were children together will know. If you and your siblings grew up on a farm in Iowa where you all arose for early morning chores, if you say "freezing toes" all your siblings will share that frigid memory of getting dressed in the icy bedroom when everyone wanted to crawl back into bed. Or if you had a dad who beat you with a hairbrush, the word *hairbrush* will be a secret signal all your siblings will hear and cringe together, remembering the beatings.

Siblings have private communication that might be just a glance or a secret word but is immediately shared. You may have different personalities and be separated by years, but your top-secret lingo and common symbols are things only siblings can truly understand. Gloria Steinem famously reminisced, "I can say 'Vernon's Ginger Ale' to my sister and she will understand." Or, it could be your oldest brother saying, "Crawl underneath the coffee table" and you and your siblings will know this is the charged phrase for Mom and Dad having another argument.

As siblings mature and grow older, there can be huge gaps and distances between the two of you, but this pivotal shared beginning of life gives you the ability to revive your relationship even if it has been separated by years and miles. One of the analogies that has been used for siblings is an air mattress. Some brothers and sisters can be pumped up whenever you need them.

Siblings are also so important to us, because they form the only relationship that lasts a lifetime. Your brother or sister is the only relative who is there—even from a distance—to see all your changes from birth to aging. You usually spent endless hours together as little kids, less as teens, sometimes only a few when you are raising your own family, then much more in midlife and into old age.

Why Reconnect with Siblings in Adulthood?
At this point, we would like you to consider the benefit of reconnecting with your sibling. In adulthood, the support of brothers and sisters can be key. Sibling relationships, as we have said, are the longest thread in your life. We start with them as kids, usually have some distance between us if we are raising our own families but can draw close again. We may have much of our adult lives left to live. In the twenty-first century, our life expectancy has doubled. Brothers and sisters can be an integral lifeline we can use to communicate and handle the issues. As we grow in maturity, siblings can share many of the burdens and the joys that take place in life.

Picture an hourglass: It is wide at the top, narrow in the middle and wide again at the bottom. Sibling interaction can be just like this. When we are kids, we see them all the time, because brothers and sisters are part of our family. In fact, we have no choice but to see them on account of the fact that we are children growing up together. But a big change happens after we grow out of our teens and siblings drift off to go to college, take jobs, get married and have kids of their own. We see our siblings less often as our twenties, thirties and forties go by, and then we find ourselves in a different part of the family hourglass. As our own children grow up, our older parents become frail, our grandchildren arrive, our lives change course and we start to interact with our siblings once more. As our lives turn, the hourglass widens, thus heralding many more reasons to seek our siblings.

Divorce is a searing transition when the support of a sibling can be a lifeboat. Siblings are also a critical support system if a parent is showing irrevocable signs of health deterioration. If we are widowed, a sibling can shore us up in this period of profound loss. There are many starring roles if you are midlife siblings. Just seeing your siblings can be a mood elevator. All these reasons show why it is key to try and repair these relationships.

Finally, like a draining hour glass, time is running out as you age. Forgiveness and reconnection have only so many seasons left. The family's play will run only so long. Death stalks the cast and will pick off the characters one by one and someday shut down the play. It is important for siblings to resolve brother and sister breaches before a chronic illness or sudden death takes a sibling and leaves the remaining one with nothing but regret.

Adult brothers and sisters can come through for us in many ways. If we move, they are the family members who most frequently help us pack, drive the moving truck and assist us in the upheaval. At parties, when we retire, the biggest toasters can be siblings. If elderly parents are moving, downsizing or relocating to warmer climates, siblings are there to help parcel out family treas-ures, sort out the collected furniture and decades of junk, working as a team to help get parents to the new location. Siblings are stellar partners in this sometimes overwhelming adult child task. If we become disabled or are ill, that sibling air mattress can quickly re-inflate, and brothers and sisters are among the first people we can call in a health care crisis, to do everything from finding answers to health problems on the Internet to finding resources to coming to our home and nursing us back to health.

A potential victim of that emptying hourglass, forgiveness is crucial as we mature. If the sand runs out before ruptures are repaired, the warped family pattern may appear in the next generation. Passing on impoverished sibling models deals a bad hand of family desolation to the next generation, passing on hurt, rage, resentment and unsutured gashes.

Making a List and Checking It Twice

After considering the infusion that realigning with your sibling in adulthood may offer, it can be vitally important to weigh both sides. To discover where the balance lies, we would like you to make a new list to measure the pros and cons of contacting your sibling and revealing your "I Hate You" story. Draw one column to catalog the positive reasons to reach out to your sibling and tell him or her your "I Hate You" story. In the opposite column, enter the negative points in bringing your "I Hate You" story out of that dark old corner. This is a very big step and the pros and cons will help tell you whether you might be poised for change or not.

Lists That the Siblings Made

Let's look at the pros and cons measured by the siblings who we discussed in earlier chapters. Angie has an "I Hate You" story about her stepsister Jennifer. In her positive column she writes that reconciling with Jennifer will make her daughter, nieces and nephew happier. She also adds that it will clear some problems in her marriage as her husband is tired of hearing the same old tale about her stepsister. Unloading the pain she has shouldered about the past, she suspects, might make her feel better. On the negative side Angie says she is still angry at her dad for marrying her step-mom and how will this change that? She also says Jennifer was the favorite when they were kids and reuniting won't fix the past.

Let's look at sister Paula's list. She writes that a plus in telling her kid sister her "I Hate You" story is it might allow Paula's little girl to be in Tammy's wedding. Paula's daughter is really upset by her mother's refusal to let her be a flower girl. So Paula puts this in the positive column. Another good reason she believes she should unearth the story is to care for herself, since she has always felt like an unwanted child. After digging in her past, Paula now under-stands she always wished she was her mom's favorite. Paula thinks maybe opening up to Tammy and getting this off her back might help her feel more loved. She thinks they might even tell their mom together and maybe her mom would love her more. Under nega-tives she lists she might have to do more to care for her aging mom if she can't keep blaming Tammy. In the minus column, what if Tammy gets so angry hearing the story she turns the other brothers and sisters against Paula? They all have a common theme, Paula muses. They all hate Tammy and what if they all started to hate Paula?

So as you consider your own story, review both lists. If you feel the positives outweigh the negatives, let us lead you to the next step. After you treat yourself more gently and give yourself incentives to reconnect, the information in this book will teach you how to write a script to tell your "I Hate You" story to your sibling and hopefully reconcile your conflicts.

☙ Chapter 8 ❧

Step Number Seven: Give Your Sibling a Chance to Hear Your Pain

Steps Toward Confiding Your "I Hate You" Story

We are going to help you move beyond insight and understanding to open the possibility of reestablishing a relationship with your sibling. This shift involves navigating a big hurdle before taking the plunge in telling your "I Hate You" story to your estranged sibling. You will be giving your brother or sister a chance to hear your recollection of that past thorny incident. If he or she agrees to meet with you, you will both have an opportunity to confront the past damage and pain and move toward a stronger relationship.

Before considering approaching your sibling, let's review the steps you have taken so far. You have penned your "I Hate You" story and moved from that place of despair to confront your pain. You chose therapeutic activities to rescript your internal sibling unrest. With a new sense of physical and mental energy you are stronger and have found the key to changing yourself. You have moved forward in your desire to gain a healthier present.

You have gained a fresh understanding of your old family system. You may have discovered rigid rules, roles and circumstances that provided the roots of your "I Hate You" story. You've surveyed your brother's or sister's family problems and roles and may have seen what led him or her to do such harm to you in the first place. With this up-to-date family portrait, you have a new picture of the present.

Studying your brother or sister today, pinpoint any type of personality traits that have changed. If he was a selfish young kid, perhaps now he's generous with his nieces and nephews. Being emotionally stronger, more sympathetic and having hope for you both to change makes you feel it is worthwhile to reconnect with your brother or sister. You have become your own lighting director, training a beam of light on a dark corner of your childhood. Recognizing his newfound illumination on your story will give both of you a chance to reestablish your relationship.

Angie Makes Her List

Let's turn back to the story of stepsisters Angie and Jennifer. Angie wonders if she can find it in her heart to confront her stepsister Jennifer. Family still unites them in adulthood. Their daughters, who are cousins, are good friends. Holidays are celebrated together, which their kids really love, even though it puts Angie in a difficult situation. Her anger at her stepsister is so visceral that she almost hates being in the same room with her.

Angie has written her "I Hate You" story and told it to a trusted friend. She looked back at the merging of her stepfamily and saw that the two clans' rules were radically different from one another. Her role as Cinderella, Angie grasps, emerged from the collision of infinitely different rules. In her mind, she has formed insights into her blended family's checkered set of laws. This has given her enough perspective and understanding to move forward.

Always rigid and cautious, Angie feels boxed in by her problems. There seems to be no way out but to care for herself. An accounting manager at work, Angie e-mails a colleague and convinces her to walk with her three days a week. She hopes to get some needed exercise and shed a few pounds, bolstering her dowdy self-image. Angie searches the company's human resources database for local stress management classes and finds a yoga class offered through her employee assistance program. She goes online and locates a stepsibling support group.

After a few months of her self-care regimen, Angie's anxiety level is notched down. She's gained enough emotional and physical stamina to list the pros and cons of reconciling with her stepsister. On the negative side, Angie feels this is a lost cause. She's mad at her dad for replacing her dearly departed mom with her nasty stepmother. There is nothing this meeting will do to silence that strangled cry of pain. Another minus is Jennifer got it all and Angie can't see how her bad memories will change by telling her story. She rages to her support group that this powwow can't change her childhood injustice. This meeting won't be a magic wand that will transform her from the ugly stepsister.

On the positive side, Angie writes that reconciling with Jennifer will be cheered by her daughter and nieces. She adds that it might improve her strained marriage as her husband grouses he's tired of hearing the same prehistoric complaints. Angie also wants to let Jennifer know how unhappy she has felt all these years. Her stepsibling support group tells her that she should throw her constant caution to the wind and get the story out of her system. Leveling with her stepsister, they tell her, will help push the reset button to lose weight, feel less anxiety and deal with her past. Her trusted friend Tomiko has encouraged Angie to get together with Jennifer, and says she is ready. By meeting Angie regularly for the last few months Tomiko has given her urgently needed support and feedback. Angie makes up her mind that the positives outweigh the negatives and she will contact Jennifer to tell her "I Hate You" story.

These past few months of taking care of herself, Angie believes, really got her to a mind-set where she can sit down and lay out her sibling tale.

Angie decides to write Jennifer a letter. An e-mail or a phone call would be too scary for her internal caution and anxiety. She checks this out with her friend Tomiko, who agrees that writing a letter is the safest way to start. So Angie writes the letter, beginning by telling her stepsister that she wants to revise their relationship. Her wish, she declares, is that the two of them can be a stronger part of their family and support their kids and themselves through the years to come. But to make that happen, she cautions, they must talk about their childhood. Some dire things happened, Angie writes, which have been keeping them apart. She ends with her goal and the reason for the meeting—to discover ways to remake their connection. She suggests a quiet early dinner at a nearby café. Then she mails the letter.

Waiting for a response, Angie calls Tomiko every day to talk about her fears. She panics that she may be opening a trapdoor. Tomiko insists that the meeting is the best thing Angie can do for herself. Her friend feels Angie is in an agitated state and needs to calm herself and feel centered. Tomiko encourages Angie to use a relaxation technique she learned in her yoga class, as well as pampering herself and continue meditating and practicing yoga, both of which Angie does regularly.

A short while later, Jennifer calls Angie and says she got the letter and it would be great to go to dinner. Jennifer shares that she went to counseling after her own divorce and then again before she was remarried. As Angie and her stepsister continue talking, Jennifer confides how she wanted desperately to help her own daughters through her divorce. Jennifer says she sought to merge the new stepsisters as smoothly as possible. Jennifer agrees that the restaurant Angie chose is perfect and they make a date to meet the following week.

What Is Your Goal in Telling Your "I Hate You" Story?
Your goal is to give peace a chance with your sibling and establish a more meaningful relationship. You want your brother or sister to be closer to you in your adult years and as you grow older. But in order to do that, you need to shine a spotlight on past events that drove you apart. Through opening these emotional tombs, your goal is to move you both to a more richly inhabited world.

Tips to Make Telling Your "I Hate You" Story Easier
Siblings are the escalator that takes us up the tiers of life. They lift us up and sometimes push us down. Your "I Hate You" story probably involves some kind of raw incident. Perhaps it is a physical altercation. Perhaps it is an emotional incident. To tell this awful story, you need to use language that will get the right message across.

Scripting Your Message
You are the messenger, but what is your message? What do you want to tell your sibling in this meeting? You want to tell the sibling you wish to reestablish a relationship with him or her that is not listless, seething or irate. After the meeting, you want to work toward forging a supportive bond that can remain for the rest of your lives. To do that, your sibling will have to listen to your "I Hate You" story. To get him or her to hear this story, you need to use words that both get your message across and invite your sibling to truly hear your words. Your message then has to be framed in language that advances those goals.

Sending Your Message—Use "I" words

"I" words help you send the message that you really own this story. This is your point of view about what happened between you and your sibling. "I" words get this ownership message across.

"I" is a pronoun that starts a sentence. An example of an "I" sentence is "I felt_____when you _____" or "I felt _____ when _____ happened."

Sentences beginning with "I" help get your sibling message heard. Why do "I" words count? Instead of your sibling simply hearing blame, "I" words allow him to focus on the story you are telling and experience, needs and wants rather than your communicating that it's the sibling's fault and then he wants to justify his needs, wants and actions.

Make the beginning of your story originate from what you remember and a description of your hurt in the past. Focus the story on your own memory of what occurred. The result will hopefully be less resentment when your sibling hears you speak and less defensiveness because you are telling him what you felt about this past incident.

Listening Skills—Hearing the Other Side

After you tell your story, you must cross over another barrier to move toward healing your sibling rift. That bridge is listening attentively to your sibling's reaction to your revelation. As we have emphasized, upon hearing your story your sibling may have a very different memory of what you believe happened. He or she may be surprised that you were so hurt by something the other may not remember. Your sibling may recall the incident but have a version of what occurred that is poles apart from yours. To achieve your goal of solving past problems then moving to the present, you have to listen to the other side of the "I Hate You" story.

Let's review some listening skills you can use. The first tool in listening is visual—acting like an engaged listener. That means your facial movements and body language should tell your sibling you are hearing what he or she says. You would not go to a movie and face the back of the theater. So look at your sibling when he or she is talking. Tune in by making eye contact. Your face gives nonverbal listening signals, so nod when you understand what is being said to you, smile when it is something pleasant and keep your face poised so the idea that you are paying attention is believable.

Be mindful of your physical position, so your body language tells your sibling you are hearing him or her. In order to look like you are listening, lean a little forward. Research shows this gives a listener a clue that you are engaged. Leaning away gives a signal that you are tuned out.

Make your posture talk. Sit facing your sibling as he or she speaks. Researchers tell us turning away from the person, even a quarter of a turn, shows a lack of interest. Imagine that your hearing is lodged in the center of your chest. To communicate with your sibling you need to illustrate your openness to the other person's point of view, so face the sibling with the center of your body as you hear his or her side of the story. If you are out having a drink together, don't hold your glass in front of your chest. Don't build blockades. Listeners see crossing your arms as a sign that they are not being heard. So if you meet at home, unfold your arms; don't pick up the pillow on the couch then plaster it in front of your chest. Move stacks of books, plants or anything that blocks the speaker's view. Let your brother or sister know there are no impediments to your receiving his or her message.

No Interrupting
If your mouth is moving, it tells the other person that you are not listening. So allow your sibling to finish his or her entire response.

Don't interrupt with counterarguments. Use receptive language by saying "I see what you are saying" or "I hear your point." This encourages your sibling's thought process, but does not limit dialogue.

Quieting Your Mind

The last skill you need to learn is quieting your mind. Buddhists tell us we have six senses and the sixth is the mind, which is rarely quiet. To fully listen, you must silence your mind, muting your inner dialogue. By thinking of counterarguments, you can't focus on what is being said. Many times our mind rattles on, like a freight train of thoughts about the past and future, blocking what we hear in the present. An open mind is a quiet mind, so concentrate on what you are hearing instead of your own internal chatter. If you find yourself drifting away, let that unfocused distraction go. Change your body position, take a deep breath, nod your head or do something to bring your mind back to the moment.

Before You Tell Your Story, Practice Your Relaxation Technique

Keep on doing and perhaps increase whatever relaxation techniques you chose to undertake (in chapter 3). If you are exercising by walking, you might walk every day instead of three times a week. If you are going to the gym, schedule an extra day. If you are taking yoga lessons, practice your exercises at home as well as going to class. This will make you healthier and emotionally stronger so that you can effectively tell your story.

Meet with Your Trusted Friend Before You Meet with Your Sibling

Before you get together with your sibling to tell your "I Hate You" story, we would like you to have a meeting with your faithful friend and review the techniques you will use to share your story. To tell the vignette of past pain, take a copy with you. First, go over the habit of using "I" words, then review listening skills. Rehearse telling your "I Hate You" story with your trusted friend, rewriting or deleting any parts that won't meet your goal of reconnecting you to your sister or brother. Make sure your story does not unnecessarily blame your sibling.

Tell the person what you have been doing to repair and heal your mental health and see if he or she can give you feedback about whether you are ready to tell your story to your brother or sister.

Contact Your Sibling

After you meet with your good friend, you are prepared to meet with your sibling. This could be a rough or calm endeavor. You can let your sister or brother know that you want to meet. You can call, write a letter, e-mail or ask privately in person—whatever makes you feel comfortable.

Invite Your Sibling to Meet

To have your sibling listen to the request and agree to meet, you need to make your invitation one he or she will accept. Start with discussing why you are meeting. In your own words, tell your sibling you want to give peace a chance and reconnect your relationship. You would like him or her to be part of your life now and in all the years to come. Explain that to do this you need to talk about your childhood and some uncomfortable things that happened that moved you apart. Follow that with your goal—to discover ways to renew your connection. This is the reason why you are contacting him or her now.

Suggest a convenient, neutral place to meet. You can select a quiet restaurant, a park or a place with fond memories from your childhood. Don't choose crowded beaches, bustling taverns or walks in freezing weather. Make sure, whatever your selection, that you will be able to hear each other and that you will both feel comfortable with the situation.

Your brother or sister may need some time to think about this, or could say he or she doesn't want to meet with you. If this happens, we will show you how you have built a healthier life for yourself in a later chapter and have already begun to heal that injury, whether you are able to tell your story to your sibling or not.

Tell Your Story

If your brother or sister agrees to meet with you, try these suggestions:

- **Be on time.**

  Don't be late. You asked your sibling to meet with you and you want him or her to hear your message. To receive that message he or she has to have trust in you. Being on time builds that trust.

- **Take a gift.**

  Gifts are wrapped in your feelings. Bring a small brightly wrapped gift for your sister or brother. This reinforces the message you want to move on to be a reliable buddy or beloved sibling through the years to come. Your gift plays that diplomatic refrain you want your sibling to hear. It could be a modest bouquet of flowers, a diminutive favorite item of his or hers or something he or she collects. Whatever you bring, make it small and have it wrapped nicely so presenting it starts the meeting on a conciliatory foot.

- **Bring your story.**

  If you feel that you might need something to lean on, bring your written story as a prompt. Explain to your brother or sister that you are nervous and may need to refer to notes to accurately tell your tale.

How to Tell Your "I Hate You" Story to Your Sibling

Share your goal for the meeting as a segue into the telling of your story. You want your brother or sister to know that your objective is to renew your relationship so you can become lifelong friends. You want to move from being estranged to being a reliable and beloved sibling through adulthood, the rich years of your midlife and on through to old age. But first you must tackle and solve old problems.

The Meeting Agenda

Start by describing your feelings in the here and now. For example, you can say you still feel sad or unloved or unimportant. Here you are explaining how this old incident still lingers in your present mind. Own up to your feelings. To diminish the possibility of your brother or sister tuning you out, use "I" words. You are telling your story from your point of view.

Then move to the past and relate what happened long ago, rupturing your relationship. You are moving to heal your internal sibling wound by allowing your brother or sister to hear your pain. To release yourself as a victim, you are sharing your memory of the past. Your message about this old painful incident will be better heard and understood if it is couched in "I" words and not full of blame. Refer to your original written story if you need to refresh your memory.

Allow Your Sibling to Tell His or Her Side of the Story

Next, it is your turn to listen to your sibling's side of the story. This meeting is a dialogue between the two of you with the goal of releasing you as the victim and your sibling as the scoundrel. To do this you need to use the listening skills we went over earlier in the chapter.

Remember, some of the engaged listener skills we discussed, including looking your sibling in the eye and facing the person, shows your sibling you are interested in that person's point of view. To telegraph that you are hearing your sibling's side with an open heart, make sure you face that person directly.

Your sibling's half of the story can vary greatly. He or she may have no memory of the past incident. Your sibling could recall what happened, but have a completely different memory of it. He or she may bring the incident to mind and be sorry for what happened. Your sibling could tell you he or she doesn't remember the story, but regrets that you have felt this way all these years, making you so unhappy and rejecting that person as a friend.

On the other hand, your sibling may tell you he or she does remember what happened and meant to hurt you because of some kind of pain you inflicted on him or her. Some siblings may not want to bridge the gap between you and will be unwilling to reconcile.

Whatever the reaction, there are two paths you can take. One is to reestablish your bond and begin releasing yourself as a victim and him or her as a culprit. After this meeting you two may agree to do that. The other path you may walk alone, because your brother or sister refuses to reestablish your sibling connection. Either way you have treated yourself with tenderness and made yourself healthy in body and mind. In essence you have forgiven yourself. Our next two chapters will give you a map to navigate either territory.

Chapter 9

Step Number Eight:
Give Siblings an Opportunity
to Establish a New Relationship

If your sibling hears your "I Hate You" story and wants to reconnect, you will now have the chance to establish a closer relationship. Whether he or she recalls the historical incident you shared in your "I Hate You" story or doesn't remember it at all, as long as he or she wants to bond with you, you can work to reject the idea of him or her as a villain and you as a victim.

Now you need to take the next steps forward with your brother or sister. To close the breach in your connection, be reassured you have already worked hard to forgive yourself. You have taken responsibility for what you are feeling and released yourself from pain.

By empowering yourself, you have ceased being the victim and begun to better handle your own emotions. Forgiveness is the transformational change you make when you become the solution to your sibling problem. You have moved forward without your sibling by your side. Let the past hurts go and journey together. We will show you how other siblings have succeeded, and you can move your renewed relationship into the present and future.

Ongoing Work on Emotional Strength

To ensure that you feel valued and strong, you need to continue your new self-care measures. An ongoing commitment to attending to yourself is an insurance policy against renewed suffering. There may be times when one of you slips and reinjures your relationship. Maintaining your own optimum strength will ensure that you access deep inner resources for healing.

You need to develop new emotional responses to nurture this reborn sibling bond. Instead of relapsing into the angry, blaming past, you need to use your awareness to stay in the here and now. In the midst of reassessing your brother or sister, you must hone talents to stay in the present to maintain your renewed link.

For years you have been on automatic, mindlessly responding to your sibling with the same old approach. Now you must strive to get beyond that pernicious habit of blame and forge a permanent tie to your sibling. To develop that caring connection you need to continually stop reliving the past and move into the present.

Building New Skills

You need nuanced attunement to your sibling to grow this new union. In order to find this ability, we would like you to make a list of five new aptitudes that can help you build that reconnection. You are developing interpersonal skills to better interact in the delicate beginning stages of your revamped connection. Perhaps you find that direct communication or compromising is tough for you, so you know you have to sharpen those to spend some new time with your brother or sister.

Stay on message and remember that you want to build a better bond now and for the rest of your life. Instead of being an irate, seething or listless sibling, you want to move toward being a buddy brother or sister. This will take abilities you may have already begun to polish through your self-care regimen. So make a pledge to cultivate those new talents and develop other positive traits to overcome any outbreak of blaming.

Do Something with Your Sibling

The next step toward a better rapport is to invite your sibling to be your partner in an activity. Suggest something you both feel comfortable doing together. Choose from the regimen you followed to make yourself healthier. For example, if you began yoga before you met with your sibling, consider asking him or her to join. Or you could both join something else, such as a dining group, volunteer organization or a gym—anything that will allow you to work or play together. You want to update your impoverished family model. Interacting can change that corrupted program. But to rewrite those codes you will also have to immediately heal the fingers that may get burned again when you reach out to work with your sibling. Resolving issues as they come up is crucial as you both go through the adult years. Many personal and family challenges as life goes on through marriage, family, midlife and aging will need a team effort. Jointly participating in an activity will give you both a chance to practice cooperation.

Learning from others who changed their old behavior can help you imitate the expertise needed to succeed in your ongoing sibling connection. If your aging parent needs care in the future, you can consider joining a caregiver group together. You can learn about the confusing gradations of blended families in a stepsibling support group. If there is an appropriate group in your area, explore the idea of a joint membership. Any support group, especially a sibling support group, will allow you to model people who have developed new aptitudes to solve problems.

Rewrite Your "I Hate You" Story

Next we would like you to rewrite your "I Hate You" story. If possible, go to the same contemplative place where you penned your original tale. This description of past suffering needs to be transformed into a present "I Love You" story. You can tell your sibling how much it means to you to reinstate your connection. Gratefulness could be offered for hearing your past story and acknowledging your pain. In your revised story you need to assure your sibling you're giving up your claim of injustice. Tell him or her how you have reframed your past complaint into this new story about how much you love him or her. You have moved from the poisonous past to the healthy present.

Create a one- or two-sentence "I Love You" mantra that will tell your sibling you have let him or her off the hook and freed yourself from your past. This simple two-sentence distillation of your "I Love You" story is something that you yourself can substitute anytime something triggers that old automatic sibling reproach in your head. That mindless, scolding chatter can be disentangled with this new "I Love You" mantra. To meet your goal of tying a tighter knot for the rest of your lives, you can add that you no longer see your sibling as an irate, seething or listless sibling and want him or her to be a buddy sibling, now and in the future. Finally, you may add the five new skills you want to use personally to make this sibling link thrive, ensuring that the connection does not slip back to an angry, destructive "I Hate You" story.

Meet Again with Your Trusted Friend

Contact your close friend, get together with her again and go over your "I Love You" story. Have her double-check your use of personal "I" words, the inclusion of a simple two-sentence mantra that you can repeat whenever you fall back to blaming and the list of five mindful skills that you want to work on to strengthen that new caring connection.

Tearing Up the Old, Sharing the New

After meeting with your good friend, contact your brother or sister. Make a new date to get together. When you meet, bring your "I Love You" story and your old "I Hate You" story. Share your new "I Love You" story with your sibling. Then, take your old "I Hate You" story, tear it up before your brother or sister and throw it in the trash. At the same time throw that "I Hate You" story into your mind's trash and empty it from the program in your head. Start fresh with both your "I Love You" story and the simple "I Love You" mantra that you can use any time your old "I Hate You" story surfaces.

Celebrate

Rituals settle quarrels and patch up the social fabric. Rites of passage are celebrated in ceremonies like baptisms, first communions, bat/bar mitzvahs and weddings. These observances mark the evolution into new stages of life. By simplifying a family transition with a ceremony, rituals control the passage of time. You have reached that plateau. To celebrate and consecrate your renewed sibling connection, we would like you to plan and take part in a ritual that will mark your reconnection and move from the blaming past to the reconnected present. You can invite your close friend and any family and friends who have supported you. It can be a dinner, a brunch, a picnic or any gathering held at a place that may be special to you and your family. If you feel comfortable doing it, read your "I Love You" story at the event. If not, just the occasion in and of itself marks the end of your sibling wars and offers a blessing to the beginning of your renewed journey together.

Glenda and Brother Chris's Story

Remember Glenda and Oscar, the married couple whose daughter, Jinx, has a cutting problem? This issue has cascaded throughout the entire family. The parents had sought low-cost sliding-scale counseling through their local Family Services office to find out what they could do as a family. An individual counselor who specializes in mental health-based teen issues was arranged for Jinx, who had also been seriously arguing with her brother Fess, reacting to her overwhelming feelings about caring for new sister Snookie when their parents worked overtime. There are issues with favoring the boy Fess over Jinx that have come out at the fault of Glenda. She harkens back to her own parents' favoring her brother Chris when Glenda was growing up in the nineteen eighties and nineteen nineties. We also talked of Oscar, and his older sister, Emily, who was used as an enforcer when he was young. This conflicting web of rules had been passed down by their original families and then stressed this family.

When their children's issues stressed the parents, they tried to work on their marriage at a retreat.

Later, Glenda, Oscar and the children are invited to Thanksgiving dinner at Glenda's parents' house and brother Chris and his wife are there as well. Chris asks Glenda to go out to coffee with him in the morning before the big dinner. To Glenda's surprise, Chris pulls out a two-page letter he had written to his sister. Explaining that their mom returned home and had a long heart-to-heart talk with him, Chris admits he took out his frustration as a kid on Glenda. He confesses he saw her as the popular sister while he was a nerd who wore glasses and buttered up the teachers to get the attention he was not getting at home. He was jealous of Glenda but really troubled and distressed by his mom and dad, who in his mind were on the verge of a divorce. He took refuge in the extra attention his mom paid him over Glenda, not realizing his mother was trying to protect him from his parents' crumbling marriage and Chris discovering his dad's infidelity.

Using "I" words, he offered an apology for tormenting his sister all those years ago and told her how sorry he was for what happened in the past. He hands her a note that tells her how much he loves her and how he wanted to make every day count now between Glenda and himself, starting with Thanksgiving. He also took another envelope out of his pocket. Glenda opened it and it was a gift certificate to stay for any weekend at a great hotel near Glenda and Oscar's home. Chris says that he and his wife will drive over to Glenda and Oscar's and watch their three kids for the weekend. Chris and his wife have two children Jinx and Fess's age and are happy to watch Snookie, the youngest.

Glenda and Chris have healed their "I Hate You" stories through the intercession of their mother. Glenda has found how extended family can be a great support in helping her meet the very critical needs of her warring children and daughter with cutting issues. Glenda accepts Chris's apology and they go back to their mom's to help cook the turkey dinner.

Angie and Jennifer's Reconnection

When Angie tells stepsister Jennifer her "I Hate You" story, they indeed discover that they can work out their relationship. Let's review how they come to such a fruitful ending.

Angie is anxious about their get-together. She girds herself by increasing the self-care tools she utilized for months to soothe the acute discomfort she suffered by digging up her "I Hate You" story. Rain or shine, she walks every day, does yoga each morning and exchanges e-mails with the members of her sibling support group on a regular basis. Angie feels like she is watching an invisible pan set to boil. She meets with an ally, Tomiko, and draws critical confidence to go forward.

Arriving at the restaurant at exactly the early dining hour she and Jennifer set, Angie hugs her stepsister and turns over a brightly wrapped box with a new summer purse inside. After settling down, she faces Jennifer with her heart and repeats the message that she wants to make their strained relationship grow stronger to support both them and their families in midlife. To make that change, Angie continues, she has to reveal some bad things that happened when they were young that have kept them apart.

After their meals arrive, Angie tells her "I Hate You" story, making sure she uses "I" words to share her take on the past. Focusing on her own center to calm herself, she enters her past painful prison. In their stepfamily, Angie states, she had to do all the dirty work while Jennifer always got off the hook. Angie believes she relived Cinderella's fate and wants Jennifer to know how gloomy and gray she felt growing up with her as a stepsister. Jennifer takes a deep breath and leans forward. As a warm smile comes across her face, she tells her side of the story.

Before her new marriage, Jennifer tells Angie, she got into counseling again to do a better job on her second shot at successful matrimony.

While listening, Angie's distracted mind starts to chatter like a chorus. She pays attention to her breath, as she has learned in yoga, and refocuses on Jennifer's words.

Jennifer shares her loathing of her mom's remarriage to Angie's dad and her childhood dream that her biological parents would get back together. She confides that she now understands that her mom failed to help her heal from the divorce. The laceration from the parental split turned into a deep scar that caused a lifelong chasm between herself and Angie. Jennifer knows she emotionally bludgeoned Angie instead of her biological mom, dad and stepdad. She gripes that her mom and Angie's father had no clue about premarital counseling before they got married. In hindsight, she understands that her stepdad was a heel to let Jennifer's mother treat Angie so poorly.

Inside her mind, Angie turns scarlet with anger, perceiving this as an attack on her family even though she is beginning to see her dad was certainly complicit. However, she shuts up the rebuttal in her head by concentrating on Jennifer's even voice.

Getting into therapy herself, Jennifer continues, she learned strategies she needed to build a new family after her own divorce. Based upon the misery she and Angie felt, she anticipated that there was going to be conflict between her kids and her new stepdaughters. A whole new emotional toolbox for softening the clash in her new stepfamily came out of counseling. She feels the most powerful tool therapy has given her is the establishment of a clear set of stepsibling rules. From counseling, she understands that her mom and stepdad had a clashing set of rules. Finally, Jennifer was able to put the past in the past. Her post-divorce and pre-remarriage therapy helped resolve her own guilt at repeating the cycle and tearing up her own young daughters' nest, then building a new one.

Looking back, Jennifer continues, she realizes her mom never asked her to do chores to make herself feel less culpable for divorcing. To assuage the guilt, her mother had Angie do all the work. Unable to repeat her mom's fatal error, Jennifer says she's so glad she learned to set the same equal, fair rules for her new stepchildren and two daughters. Reaching her hand out to Angie, she says she is so sorry that she suffered all those years and she hopes that they could start to make up for the misery she endured.

They grin shyly at each other across the table and Angie feels drained but strangely calm. She and Jennifer established a connecting line, but need to fuse their sisterhood together and replace the severed sibling cable. To start fashioning that lifeline, they decide to do an activity together but leave the specifics open.

Angie Meets with Her Trusted Friend

Angie goes home and calls Tomiko, asking her to get together the following afternoon. After hearing what happened, her girlfriend suggests that she ask Jennifer to join in one of her therapeutic activities. Thinking about Jennifer, Angie decides to see if she wants to join her stepsibling support group. This might be a way to build a better sister bond. In an e-mail reply, Jennifer says that she is very open to this. She wants to forge this new connection to end the suffering between them, as this would also help her be a better stepmom to her stepdaughters.

Angie Chooses Five Skills to Reconnect

Angie makes a list of five skills that will help her and Jennifer nurture their new tentative tie. On her part, she knows her own blaming could erupt again. Unless she makes more changes in herself, she might end up reliving her anger and hostility toward her stepsister.

Angie thinks long and hard and decides that one skill she needs to work on is flexibility to counter her very rigid nature. Stepping into someone else's shoes is another skill she feels she needs to master. Angie understands that she really never knew Jennifer or understood what she was going through as a kid. She adds to her list of new talents to be learned the concept of staying in the present, not the past. Rather than morphing back into Cinderella or Little Orphan Annie, Angie needs the skill to be the in-control human resources person she is in the here and now. Kindness is another skill she knows she needs to learn. Angie started with yoga, but she plans on pampering herself by going to the beauty salon and having her nails done frequently. Finally Angie knows that she must end her jealous feelings that everyone is better off than she is. Looking at her life now, she knows it's finally pretty full and she needs to see her glass that way, not always half empty and jealous of someone else's brimming glass.

Angie Writes Her "I Love You" Story

Angie goes to her home office, the place she wrote her original "I Hate You" story. Her desk is perfectly organized with each file in place, making her feel calm and in control. She realizes that in this rewrite she needs to jettison her claim of injustice held against Jennifer all these years. Opening her laptop, she creates a new document to rewrite her "I Hate You" story. In the first few lines, she admits that she has been holding Jennifer responsible for decades in regards to injuries inflicted on both of them as children. She continues by stating how she understands that Angie's dad and Jennifer's mother had no idea there was such emotional fallout after they remarried and in their era, counseling was not frequently sought out. As remarried parents, they failed to help Jennifer and Angie through the rocky formation of their new blended family.

In addition, Angie continues that her dad and Jennifer's mom never understood they were imposing two radically different sets of rules about chores in the new family. As a result, Angie felt like Cinderella, while Jennifer became the evil stepsister. Unfortunately, Angie says, she had no fairy godmother. She ends by telling Jennifer that she is accepting her now as a buddy sibling, not the irate, demanding stepsister she thought she was.

She fashions a two-sentence "I Love You" mantra that releases them both from their chaotic childhood prison and makes a vow to treat their children more lovingly than they were treated in the future. She tells Jennifer, "I will love you as my stepsister, putting in the past our childhood pain. I vow to treat my kids, your children and your stepchildren with an equal amount of love and support."

Finally she ends the letter by revealing the five new skills she will hone to guard their relationship. Angie now believes they can make their stepsister bond grow stronger to support both of them and their families as they grow older. They have worked hard to hash out the troubles from their childhood that left them at an icy distance. Finally she believes she is loved by Jennifer.

Angie then writes that she is giving up her claim of injustice and throwing it in the wastebasket. She is releasing Jennifer as the villain and herself as the victim in the real fairy tale. After printing her "I Love You" story, she goes out shopping for a fashionable version of glass slippers.

Wearing her new bejeweled pumps, Angie has tea with Tomiko and reads Angie's fresh "I Love You" story. She wants to make sure she has used "I" words in what she has written. After Tomiko's approval and support, the stepsisters get together again in Angie's home office, where she has a cozy couch and has built a fire in the fireplace. Angie reads her rewritten "I Love You" story. She has a copy of the old "I Hate You" story. They rejoice in the moment. Angie takes her "I Hate You" story, tears it up in front of Jennifer and then tosses it into the flames.

Ted and John

Although he started to take care of himself by joining a fitness program at the local gymnasium, Ted saw the damage from his brother was so deep he needed counseling. He worked on changing his own family patterns, seeing the parental missteps that led to John injuring him as a kid. For a few months, Ted attended the therapy sessions, and, at the suggestion of the marriage and family therapist, joined a meditation group. He knows he has to work on moving into the moment to stop getting stuck in the past with the saga of the jagged glass. Meditation will help him get there, he believes.

Ted Tells His "I Hate You" Story

After many counseling sessions, Ted finally feels strong enough to tell his "I Hate You" story. He e-mails John a request to meet, with the simple message that he wants to work on improving their relationship and talk about what has stood in the way all these years.

John's happy to get together and they meet at a baseball field where they both used to play Little League baseball. Ted brings his "I Hate You" story, written with "I" words. The counselor helped him write it and he practiced it with him.

Ted fumbles giving a gift he knows John will like—two hard-to-get tickets to the annual homecoming game. They sit down on a bench, and Ted launches into his story. John turns pale while Ted talks. At the end John tells his brother he's glad he was able to finally talk about his feelings because what happened has really upset him as well. He tried to forget what he did, because he's so ashamed. Ted, who is a social worker, shares how he went back and talked to their aunt and uncle about what really occurred and now knows that John was harmed by his actions. He explains that he felt cheated. He had to forsake after-school sports, because he had to be a fill-in father for the one who had abandoned them both. Their mom, Ted now understands, put too much pressure on John babysitting Ted, but it all started when their dad left all three of them. After they talk, Ted and John each give each other a big hug and agree to get together again.

Following the encounter, Ted has an appointment with his therapist. He confides that the meeting went well, but he has some fears. What if John turns back into the same loud, bossy person he was when they were kids and hurts him again? The therapist says that Ted has to work on taking responsibility for what he is feeling and learn to be in control of his own emotions. John can be bossy, but Ted can choose not to be pushed around. Learning new skills to be forceful, no matter what his brother does, will allow Ted to solve any problem he runs into in their new sibling friendship.

Putting John on a Forgiveness Payment Plan

Ted's therapist proposes creating a forgiveness payment plan for his brother. She suggests instead of fully forgiving John, Ted put the relationship into low gear for a trial period. After several months, if Ted feels he can trust John, he can consider that his brother has passed the trust test and Ted can buy the entire plan resolving their severed bond. This sounds like a good deal to Ted.

The counselor suggests asking John to do an activity together to revise their impoverished family model and teach them to start working together. This will help Ted start to dissolve his automatic blame response in his journey to achieve forgiveness for John. If John agrees to join in an activity, after several months of together-ness, Ted will be able to see whether or not John treats him as an equal without slipping back into being the loudmouth, domineer-ing brother. Even if he does, Ted can see if he has learned the skill of not allowing himself to be pushed around. If John is not always the bossy bully from the past and, when he does slip back, Ted is strong enough not to be the victim, they will have made this sibling transformation. Then, the counselor proposes, Ted can offer full forgiveness, ending the payment plan.

Ted's Five New Skills to Stop Being a Victim

The counselor proposes that Ted come up with a list of five new skills he will practice during the trial period. Ted says he needs to learn to be more assertive and get better at expressing his feelings.

The therapist proposes he join a club where he can do some public speaking. Building confidence in public speaking might push Ted out of his comfort zone. Ted's artistic talents are something he has never really worked on, the therapist suggests, and Ted may get better at articulating his feelings by taking an art class.

Ted says he knows he's a pessimist and has a hard time believing that any of this is going to work. They discuss his catastrophic thinking that the worst is always going to happen. The therapist suggests he could work on optimism by joining a local mentoring program. She knows that John has always been domineering and she thinks Ted can learn the power of positive change by aiding less fortunate children. Agreeing, he sees modeling this behavior would help his sons and himself. Ted still suffers from his father deserting him and would like to help another child who doesn't have a responsible, caring parent in his or her life.

Ted now feels it's important to be a fairer dad and a better husband. He vows to continue to take time with both his boys and not leave one in the care of the older child. He and his wife also decide to go away for a weekend and renew their relationship. A child of divorce, Ted does not want his kids to end up in the same situation he and his brother endured.

The forgiveness layaway plan, coupled with joining an organization to help children and attending an art class all appeal to Ted. The idea of public speaking still makes him very nervous, however, but he says he will give it a try. He is committed to working on his parenting and marriage.

Ted feels that John might be most open to going to the gym with him. His brother has grumbled about putting on a few pounds and would like to get into better shape. John welcomes the idea and the brothers start going to the gym together twice a week.

Six months later, Ted returns for his weekly session with the counselor. He tells the therapist he and John have been going to the gym together and feel like they have conquered many barriers. Ted has learned to let go of John's bombastic personality. They have both lost over ten pounds with John hitting the mark first, which they both laughed about. Ted's jitters at speaking publicly have since been quieted by the group he joined to practice public speaking. He feels he has conquered his paralyzing fright while building confidence in being assertive. He also loves the applause he receives.

The best part is his mentor, who has encouraged Ted to get better with each speech. He also has become a mentor himself to a lonely fourteen-year-old boy whose dad is absent, as Ted's was. This has helped him act like the older brother he always wanted John to be and indeed is right now. His catastrophic fears about his new sibling connection were unfounded. He himself has become a model for helping John re-craft their relationship. John and Ted's connection is now at the point where Ted believes he can fully forgive his brother and throw away the payment plan. The six-month trial period has built Ted's trust in his ability to be more assertive and express what he feels. Art class, Ted feels, has given him the ability to express his feelings in a creative way. Being more assertive and more in touch with his intuitive side has helped him with his marriage and parenting. Ted is ready to rewrite his "I Hate You" story into an "I Love You" story.

Rewriting Ted's "I Hate You" Story
Ted redrafts his "I Hate You" story and the therapist reads it. After going to the gym one day Ted asks John if they can drive by their old house where teenage John sat Ted down on a floor of broken glass. Sitting in the car across the street, Ted pulls out his "I Love You" story and tells it to John. He focuses on the two-sentence "I Love You" mantra and tells John he no longer sees him as the villain and has freed himself from the label of victim. He knows now that

John was only a kid, who was under a lot of pressure from their very overwhelmed mom. He is letting that past mistake, made in the yard across the street, go so he and John can have a buddy connection in the present and future to help their families and their aging mom. Grinning, John pulls out the tickets to the big game. "Go with me, buddy," John proposes. That's finally fine with Ted.

Chapter 10

Step Number Nine: Surround Yourself With Love Even Without Your Sibling

When Ginger finally decides to tell her brother Bobby her "I Hate You" story, the siblings agree to meet at a park where they used to play as kids. Arriving a few minutes early, Ginger has her "I Hate You" story tucked in her purse in case she needs a prompt. A small wrapped package holding a flash drive for Bobby lies in her pocket. Her brother always grouches about needing more backup for his computer files.

Finally, a huffing Bobby plops onto the bench. His face bunches up as he says, "This better be good." Smiling, Ginger hands Bobby her gift. Tearing off the rich purple paper, he asks what she wants from him. She takes a deep breath and answers she really hopes to feel closer to him and build a better relationship for the rest of their lives. However, first she needs to talk about some things that really bother her. "What are you talking about?" Bobby rasps, crumbling the wrapping paper in his hand.

Ginger focuses on the "I" words and repeats how much she wants to rekindle their relationship. Feeling on edge but confident, she explains that she thinks she could be closer to Bobby if they worked together to share their mom's increasing care. Reaching back in the past, she makes clear how she feels not sharing chores started when they were kids. They had no control over their parents' rules, she now understands. Ginger then launches into her "I Hate You" story, focusing on their dad forbidding her to go away to college while young Bobby snickered. Ginger switches to the present saying the family rule about gender still seems to apply. From her vantage point, she does most of the work for their mother and would appreciate more of a division of labor. Ginger emphasizes that this is her opinion and she now wants to listen to her brother's point of view.

Bobby stands up. His nose flairs as he roars that he has no memory of Ginger ever asking their dad if she could go away to college. In fact, he recalls that she spent her childhood chasing after boys and taking nothing but easy classes. Even though he loves her, he coldly warns, she's got to admit she's not as smart as he is. Bobby storms off, throwing the flash drive his sister bought for him into the pond along the way. Ginger is left sitting alone in a square of light, watching Bobby disappear toward the busy street. Her brother did not apologize for being heartless about their dad's ruling that Ginger couldn't go to college. After she shared her thoughts, Bobby abruptly rushed away with no commitment to help out more with their mother's care. Ginger is left empty handed—or is she?

The Power of Forgiveness

After you tell your "I Hate You" story, what if your sibling is not repentant and has no interest in reconciling? The answer to this is, even without an apology, you have transformed your life. Absolution is just for you and does not have to involve your brother or sister. Forgiveness is the emotional calm you feel when you take responsibility for what you are feeling. It is the power you give yourself when you stop being a victim and start being a person who controls your own emotions. Forgiveness is the peace that surrounds you when you end your own suffering and become the solution to your sibling problem. You have begun all of these steps even without an apology.

Through bringing your "I Hate You" story to the surface, you have started making major alterations in yourself. You have moved to the present where you have chosen to be a healthier and happier person. In your transformation you have gained a whole arsenal of tools to change yourself. You have learned skills to make your body healthier and your mind more serene.

What You Already Have Without an Apology

If your sibling listens to your request to patch things up and refuses, you still have come a long way on your journey to gain insight into the roots of your sibling "I Hate You" story. You have become attuned to your own health and developed an appetite for your personal happiness. You have turned into your own teacher.

Through bringing her "I Hate You" story to the surface, Ginger has put a spotlight on the archaic rules from her family of origin. As a kid, her family edicts left her doing all the housework and having no choice but to skip college. Her old impoverished operating system is still at work, but she is now installing updated programs. These new rules say Ginger can go to college. She has other new choices.

As an adult, she now understands how blindly she accepted the overwhelming role of the sole caregiver in her family. She has fixed her expired program. She can now delegate some of the parent care to others. Her family's old rule that boys have the key to every door while girls are locked outside is now obvious to Ginger. Awakened to new choices, she now rejects the paralyzing gender bias she inherited and perceives the emotional toll all these old operating systems have taken on her. In fact, through creating her "I Hate You" story, Ginger has really discovered how frustrated, depressed and bristling with resentment she has been her whole life.

Forgive Yourself by Beginning to Heal Yourself
In spite of Bobby's refusal to acknowledge either her childhood
wound or her overwhelming caregiver burden, Ginger has begun
to forgive herself. She has made the choice to hurt less and heal
more. Feelings about her brother, denied for decades, have been
unearthed. She has named those thoughts and written them down.
Telling her trusted friend, Martha, and sharing her story speeds
Ginger further down the road to coping with her inner turmoil.

Translating our emotions into words and then revealing them to
confidants launches us into the world of caring for ourselves. Getting
the direction and backing of another person or group helps us feel
less isolated and more part of the clan. Whether they be family or
friends like Martha, close people we trust offer us a safe haven by
agreeing to be an ongoing support system to midwife our change.

Bring Yourself Out of the Past Into the Present
Even without Bobby's apology or committed support, Ginger has
brought herself out of the past, where her "I Hate You" story had
her stuck in her own cycle of pain and denial. She named the pain
in her "I Hate You" story, switching on a light in that darkness. She
has launched herself into the present, where she can move forward
with her life. By saying her sibling story out loud, Ginger unlocked
the cell that kept her mired in the past, then walked out that prison
door. By transforming herself she tore down the barricades of old
in order to change. Ginger found forgiveness by releasing herself
as a victim, even if she has not reconciled with Bobby. She
commuted her own life sentence.

The Healing Power of Self-Help
Though Bobby hurled her gift into the pond and denied Ginger's
story, she is making herself a healthier and happier person. Numb

to her childhood suffering, as we often are when we were mis-treated as kids, Ginger faced her pain head-on. By finally admitting to the darkness of her childhood, she wrote her "I Hate You" story. Seeing that her emotional damage is threaded through to her present, she decides to change. No longer anesthetized, Ginger chose a regimen of self-care to cauterize her wound. Dedicating herself to her own health, she chooses five therapeutic activities.

Her doctor tells her high blood pressure is stress-related, so Ginger joins a stress management group at her local medical clinic. She hopes to get off her blood pressure medication by practicing the techniques learned in the class. The new writers group Ginger joins encourages her to take tentative steps to pen a historical fiction novel based on the Armenian genocide. This en-couragement boosts her sense of self-worth.

By journaling each day, she sees that she is still cast in a pigeon-holed role by taking on all of her mom's care. After attending her support group for several weeks, Ginger realizes that she is in a state of caregiver burnout. By setting herself up as a victim, she has allowed herself to suffer in the present. Through listening to other members who have hired caregivers for needed respite, she grabs that new choice and signs up for a care provider. Ginger stops going to her mom's house every day after work. With her free time, she gets a massage, makes an appointment for a stylish new hairdo and enrolls in an creative writing class at the local college. Ginger has chosen five transformative activities to care for herself.

Turn Off the Endless Spigot
In chapter 4, we saw that Ginger's mind was like a broken spigot. She poured blame on her brother Bobby each night that she single-handedly cared for their mom. As she cooked her mom's dinner, a constant rant played in her head faulting Bobby for never helping

with their mom's care. As the water boiled, her blood pressure rose with an internal chorus of blame.

Now that she has employed a caregiver to come to her mom's house and help with the chores, giving Ginger some time for her own children and needs, she can then turn off the faucet. She's stanched the never-ending stream of blame in her mind. The few evenings she stops by her mom's, instead of hearing the same old internal racket about Bobby, she listens to a new personal resolution that she has learned in her stress management class. That mantra is to treat her children equally regardless of gender. When the same old blame game plays in her mind, she changes her own conversation and repeats this intention about her children. This new resolve helps control her endless blaming and soaring blood pressure. Ginger is rewriting her "I Hate You" story.

Safeguarding Against Future Damage

After you tell your "I Hate You" story, even if your sibling is not open to reconciling, you have pried open that past tomb of harm. You can now see the damage that played out in your family of origin. You have gained insight into your family's broken operating system and can see that you need to protect the next generation. Through that knowledge, you can safeguard against repeating that hurt and pain in your own family. To protect her own kids, Ginger made the resolution to treat her children equally with no regard to gender.

Then Ginger inventoried her judgments with her two daughters and son and decided to permanently sweep out her own sexual bias. She deleted her parents' rule that only girls do housework and Ginger's son and daughters do an equal number of chores after school. Her older daughter loves biology, so Ginger and her husband send her to a local university science camp created to encourage girls to choose a career in that field. Her younger daughter shows a real talent in school woodshop. Ginger's husband owns a construction company, so rather than box their daughter in a stereotypic female role, Ginger and her husband put a red carpet down for their daughter's entrance into what was originally considered to be a boy's world. Finally all her kids are on track to go to college and Ginger and her husband encourage them all to get higher education. Ginger has moved from the negative past to a positive present by focusing equally on her son and two daughters. She has altered her family pattern so her own children won't repeat the past, only to recycle it to yet a newer generation to repeat, creating an endless dysfunctional loop. She has done all this even though her brother Bobby denies her "I Hate You" story.

Protect Yourself Against Future Injuries

By seeing the bad choices your original family made, you can protect yourself from future injuries even without your sibling's renewed friendship. Through her support group, Ginger is able to see what the future would hold for her as the beleaguered solo caregiver. She employed an aide to come on weekdays, so she can have help tending to her mom. She learns, through listening to fellow family caregivers, that her mom's needs will surely increase, risking the possibility of more stress, high blood pressure and the constant cycle of blaming Bobby.

She knows that she will have to get more help for her mom's increased care requirements. A member of her caregiver support group tells her about an elder-law attorney and she consults with one. Ginger realizes that if she has no help from her family system, she will have to hire more homecare as her mother ages. The lawyer, with her mom's permission, looks at her parents' estate and finds out there is enough money for increased future care. She also discovers that her mom has a long-term care policy that will pay for some of this support. In taking these steps, Ginger has begun to protect herself against future overload. She is beginning to change her lifelong pattern. By preparing to care for her mother in the future, she is treating herself with new tenderness. Through her past patterns, she understands that if she does not nurture herself, she may still be stuck absorbing all the future parent problems. She has catered to her own future interest, even without reconciling with her brother.

Ginger's Rich Life Without Her Sibling

Ginger has made many changes in herself, but those modifications have not altered her relationship with Bobby. Although this is a sad development, if you, like Ginger, try but are unable to repair the sibling relationship, it is not an ending but a new beginning. If the changes you accomplished include creating a bigger circle of friends and larger networks, these support systems are a major revision of your life, even without your sibling.

Ginger doesn't have the support of Bobby, but she does have the reinforced support of her family and friends. She joined a caregiver support group, where she has gotten great ideas for reducing her stress and increased her own personal time to nurture herself and her own family by hiring care providers. Her new writing group has encouraged her dream of being an author. Ginger's own family, including her daughters, son and husband, have rallied around her. She and her husband have changed the ruinous rules from Ginger's past. Her friend Martha has listened to Ginger's revelation and supported her as she climbed the steep steps to transform herself while confronting her "I Hate You" story. The stress management group at the medical center has guided her in reducing her blood pressure and learning to substitute a healing resolution every time her mind begins to blame Bobby. She hopes to use this newfound strength to eventually control her blood pressure herself without using medication. Ginger has surrounded herself with the backing of many people who have helped her change, all without her brother. They have continued to hear her pain and smoldering rage toward Bobby and her family of origin and have helped her change this destructive train of thought. Her support network is pointing to a path that will guide her in ministering herself in the present. Ginger has taken a proverbial photograph of her family and friends that does not include Bobby and it's a great picture.

The Cycle of Revenge Must End with You

Ginger's "I Hate You" story revealed considerable suffering from her past. She focused on her unrepentant brother, who was granted privileges and choices she never had. But only Ginger can give herself those new options. By healing herself, she can take back her power. However, in order to do this, she made a critical new move. To hold onto her power, Ginger can't plunge into a cycle of revenge. If she sets out to get even with Bobby for not reconciling, she will always remain a victim while Bobby will continue to be the perpetrator of pain. To rub out this endless payback cycle, she has to tear up her "I Hate You" story. Ginger needs to heal herself, move on with her life and not remain stuck in a world of accusations. Through education and social interaction, Ginger has begun to see new choices and change herself. She has grasped her own power to control her alternatives and they don't include retribution.

She does not want to give that power away again, as she did when she assumed the overwhelming burden of her mother's care. So, in turn, she hires a caregiver to give her some help on weekends and evenings. When she was a child, she had no choice but to accept the gender inequality of her family rules. Now, as an adult, she has choices and treats her son and daughters equally. She has the option not to be a victim and not to make Bobby the villain, so she seeks no retribution for his rejection.

Even though Bobby has walked out on her, Ginger has to stop blaming him. By not holding her brother responsible for both her past injury and her present anger, she prevents him from controlling her emotions.

In Ginger's "I Hate You" story, Bobby was also a kid. He had no power, just like Ginger. Although Bobby's actions have seemed uncaring, by continuing to hold him responsible for the past, even after he refused to reconcile, her endless blaming will keep Ginger stuck in exactly the same, awful system from which she is trying to escape. Even though Bobby refused to become a "buddy" brother, denied her past wound and rejected any part of their mother's care, Ginger needs to forgive him. This pardon will ensure that Ginger keeps her power to change herself. It will ensure that she can make the choice of self-forgiveness without being mired in the endless cycle of reproach. If she stays wedged in the cycle of retribution, a new wound will fester where the old one was. This latest cycle of vengeance will create a brand new script for a revised "I Hate You" story about settling scores. So when Bobby walked away from Ginger, leaving her alone on the bench as the ducks hid on the other side of the pond, she made a choice. She could forgive her brother or start a new round of self-inflicted pain. She decided to forgive.

Ginger chooses to understand that Bobby is unable to change their impoverished family system, but she can. These rules created by their parents were innocently accepted by young Bobby as the recipe to life. As an adult, he still can't see the failed formula. Ginger's newfound compassion comes from all her therapeutic activities. She has transformed herself from a victim into a woman with options. She has a choice to hire care if Bobby will not help her. She also has an option to not pursue vengeance. She makes the decision to have compassion for her sibling's inability to change the old family rules.

Being a Sibling is Voluntary—
Taking Care of Yourself and Being Healthy Is Not

As we said earlier, as adults, having a sibling relationship is voluntary. When you were kids, you had no choice but to be in the same house. As an adult, however, you can always choose not to see your sibling. Bobby has made a choice not to have a supportive relationship with Ginger. She, on the other hand, can make a decision to accept that preference. She has healed enough to know she is a strong person without Bobby.

If your sibling rejects your request to build a closer, more loyal relationship, you can accept that option if you have worked to build a self that is in good physical and mental shape. When you reach out to your extended family and friendship system, you can count on them to be a buttress in your life. If you have constructed a new set of supportive connections, you can use them as additional beams of support and social networks to help you better balance your days, with or without your sibling.

Rewriting Your "I Hate You" Story

Even if your sibling has not acknowledged your pain, we would like you to rewrite your original "I Hate You" story. To do this, make a list of all the family and friends in your present support system. Include your close ally who first heard your "I Hate You" story and backed you through all the steps you took to try to reconcile with your sibling. Add all the social networks or support groups you have joined to care for yourself. After you have your list, practice your relaxation techniques every day for a week.

Then take this list to a contemplative place. Use that calm and supportive space to rewrite your "I Hate You" story. Start your revision with several paragraphs telling yourself all the steps you have taken to propel yourself into a healthier lifestyle. Include all the therapeutic activities that you have undertaken to heal yourself. Write about how you have changed as a result of your own self-care. Then write a few paragraphs about how you felt when you moved into the present and finally felt strong enough to tell your sibling your "I Hate You" story.

Continue by describing what happened when you exposed your "I Hate You" story to your sibling and how he or she reacted to your revelation.

Next we would like you to write about what you wish had happened between you and your sibling. Ginger writes she wishes that Bobby had been a kinder, more supportive brother in the past and present. Ginger is not stating what she demands to happen with rules that she cannot enforce. She can't change the past and she can control only herself, not Bobby. She can only say what she wishes. So write down what you wish had happened in your story.

Finally, write a few paragraphs about what you have done to heal your sibling wound without your brother or sister's support. Include your refurbished family nest absent of your sibling. Write a few paragraphs about how you have accepted your sibling for who he or she is for now and how you hope that at some time in the future the seeds you have planted may grow into reconciliation and make your wish come true. Describe how in spite of his or her present feelings you have healed your own wound and will be there for your own children, family and friends now and in the future. There is always your internal camera you can use to take a new picture that puts your sibling back in the frame. If the hurt is too deep and you still feel like seeking revenge, consider contacting a therapist, as Ted did, to help you work through your feelings and your pain. You have taken many steps to heal yourself, and entering therapy is yet another curative step to healing your sibling wound.

Tell Your Rewritten Story to Your Trusted Friend

Next we would like you to make a new date with your good friend and read your rewritten "I Hate You" story. Bring a copy of your original "I Hate You" story. After you read the first "I Hate You" story, have a ritual cleansing and tear it up. Whether you shred it, crumple it up, delete it, rip it to shreds or burn it (safely), you must destroy the old story. And with that, empty the trash in your mind as well. You have worked hard to heal yourself, even without the offender acknowledging your past or present pain. You are releasing your brother or sister as the violator and yourself as the victim. In fact, you are clearing the negative balance on the family ledger.

Celebrate

Since you have forgiven and healed yourself by emptying the negative emotions in your mind and letting your feelings about the wrongdoer go, you can now celebrate. Plan a dinner, a picnic or a gathering for your trusted friend and other key people who have supported you. Rituals guide us through transitions and you have shifted from being a victim with an "I Hate You" story to a healed person who has shredded that tale. Count the blessings that are your emotional buoys. By creating this rite you are celebrating your own release from pain and suffering. Hold the event once a year to celebrate the ending of your "I Hate You" story. Eventually your sibling might even join the celebration.

Chapter 11

Step Number Ten: Revive Midlife Sibling Relationships

Remember that sibling hourglass that we talked about earlier? Midlife once more pours itself into the bulbous end of that spectrum. If you and your siblings are still estranged, do not despair. The intimacy of young sisters and brothers can be reclaimed in middle age and as you grow old. At the third act on the family stage, you've gone past act one of childhood and act two of raising your own families. At that point, you can use those profound childhood links to increase the joy in our lives and help heal the wounds with which you may suffer as you age.

By mending that bond, you and your sibling can now become best friends. Raised in the same environment, he or she knows everything about you from childhood. That secret language of siblings gives an on-the-spot sense of understanding between one another. One word to your brother or sister may bring back a whole chapter from your past. There is no one else like that in your world. Your sibling knows your life from the beginning and as you grew up. He or she comes installed with your preprogrammed history.

Positive Stages of Midlife

Ending sibling discord gives one a new lease on life. During midlife, many have raised their children, who are now becoming adults themselves. Then comes the birth of grandchildren, preceded by showers and followed by christenings, confirmations, bar mitzvahs or junior high graduations that mark the third leg of life. Once you have breached the fortress mentality of your "I Hate You" story, your midlife sibling can bear witness to these key phases of your grandchildren's lives. He or she can help you sanctify the rituals saluting the newest generation. She supplements and enhances your role as an elder in the ceremonies that mark family passages. Siblings attend engagement parties, baby showers, housewarmings and graduations. They are both audience and actors in the ceremonies that mark the passage of time in your own adult children's hourglasses. You, in turn, can now do the same for your sibling's family. This refurbished causeway allows both your generation and the next to fluidly celebrate all family passages.

Midlife opens new vistas. Unfettered from the bonds of child rearing, you have more time for hobbies, trips and social networking. A reknit rapport creates an instant fellow traveler, online friend, hobbyist or a welcome drop-in visitor at your empty nester home. There is no one who can share activities in midlife like a sibling with whom you share a renewed connection. If you have other brothers and sisters, this rekindled warmth melts the ice so all siblings can get together. Family reunions can have decreased chances for drama, because you and your sibling are no longer foes.

Patched Up Sister Connections Reap Midlife Well-Being

Well-being in midlife is greatly enhanced when you have a tighter sibling attachment. If two sisters have resolved their struggles, they have repaired more than their bond. Researchers report the greatest degree of intimacy and unconditional love among sisters. Remember the six types of siblings we discussed (chapter 2)? If you have repaired the ropes between you and your sister, you have also forged the strongest friendship of any sibling pair. Women are hardwired to share and support. If you have mended your connection with your sister, you have strengthened the ties with your best friend. Women are the kin keepers of society. In middle age, they are most often the organizers of celebrations marking familial passages. You and your reconnected sister can provide support for each other by organizing the myriad details of midlife rituals, like christenings, weddings and retirement parties. Genealogy becomes more important in midlife as you reach back to find your ancestral roots. Sisters are frequently the creators of lineage charts and together you can spend endless hours following the branches of the family tree.

Men benefit from the reconnection of sisters in midlife as well. Researchers have found that men in their middle years have greater senses of psychological assurance if they have a sister. So if a brother and sister were estranged, a respliced bond allows that brother to be happier in middle and old age. Why is this true? We believe women have deeper emotional landscapes and naturally work together in groups. Having a sister creates a better chance for a brother to be brought into all the family activities of middle age, oftentimes orchestrated by sisters. All those midlife ceremonies usually have a female as the event planner, and she will most certainly include the newly befriended brother in her plans.

Becoming the Air Mattress

After forty, you may see the onset of many chronic health concerns. Now that you have sparked your sibling connection, you can be that proverbial air mattress for each other. If one of you becomes ill, the other can move quickly to the other's side to take care of kids still at home, be a patient advocate with the health care system, stay by a bedside or make meals when the ill person returns home. Much like that air mattress, you can suddenly inflate, support your sibling and deflate when the crisis is over. This kind of support system could not have happened if your "I Hate You" story still existed.

Reconnected Siblings in the Negative Stages of Midlife

Just as the rebirth of your sibling friendship gives you a partner to mark the ritual family entrances, this repaired schism can also help you weather life's exits. As you move through midlife, there often are wrenching losses. Divorce, which tears relationships apart at any age, occurs most frequently between the ages of forty-five and fifty-four, while historically it used to spike among younger married couples. Having a sibling to support you when marriage crumbles can be a great blessing and a positive consequence of the dissolution of your "I Hate You" story. Siblings can stand by you through the dissolution emotionally, backing you as you recover from this devastating ending. Some midlife couples not only undergo their own marital tribulations, but suffer doubly if their adult children's marriages split up as well, which is a serious problem in our culture. A reforged sibling connection can give major sustenance as you support your own adult children and/or grandchildren through the scathing effects of marital break-ups.

When a spouse dies in midlife, it is a major emotional blow. Having a sister has been shown to be one of the greatest supports to a woman in widowhood. If a woman has reconnected with a sister by ending an old sibling battle, her chances of better coping with a spouse's death are multiplied. Brothers also can be a great support. If a man is widowed and reconnects with his sister, his widowerhood becomes emotionally easier to cope with as well.

Reunited Siblings and Parent Care

As parents age, many modifications must be made to their lives. One adjustment may be downsizing their home. Adult children become deeply involved in this transition, as a smaller home or residence near adult children or where weather is warmer needs to be located. In taking apart the family homestead, you are literally editing memories. Valuable family heirlooms or not-so-priceless nontitled property, loaded with family recollections, must be divided or sold by family members. This can be a wrenching move for the older person but equally hard for adult siblings. Many family wars are fought over Mom's salt-and-pepper shaker collection or Dad's bowling balls.

There is potential for great loss when getting rid of personal belongings, furniture, pictures and even clothes, because they represent safety and family history. The crux of the sorting is not just what will be moved and discarded but also getting through the trauma of leaving the family's past. Adult siblings are decimating their former safe space by determining what items go and what items stay. This proves to be fertile ground to reignite contentious sibling wars.

If you and your brother or sister have rebuilt your relationship, you can both help your parents go through all the tough steps of relocation, ensuring that the fight over Dad's record collection or Mom's kitchen supplies will be resolved without new blood drawn.

Aging parents begin to show cracks in their ability to live independently as adult children reach middle age. As health crises arise, midlife siblings can often find themselves gathered to resolve an older parent's emergency. At this point, siblings need to regroup as a team, something that most likely hasn't happened since childhood. By fixing that spurned sibling split, you both can support your parent as a unit, not as cackling sidelined rivals.

Parent care can be overwhelming, unplanned and unexpected. There is no rulebook out there that warns families of the new developmental stage, prompting them to prepare.

As men and women go through midlife, crises often erupt in their parents' lives. Hovering over their ill parent with no family disaster plan in place, siblings can snarl at each other instead of working as a team. In these instances, one brother or sister often takes on the role of caretaker and feels overwhelmed with little support from the others. Your repaired sibling bond gives you instant team members to both mobilize and make the best plans for caring for parents.

Conflicts in handling the needs of your aging parents can open the grafted skin of your old sibling gash. You may have healed the old injury, but when you and your sibling are faced with the needs of a frail parent, you become angry and divided again. If a brother and sister have reunited after a long lapse, gender challenges are frequently reignited. Gender dominates all aspects of the caregiving agenda and sisters bear the biggest load in aging parent support. If a brother expects a sister to shoulder most of the eldercare, this causes renewed conflicts. If one sibling lives far away and the other close, the local sibling often becomes the sole caregiver. A sister or brother who is widowed may be expected to shoulder the caregiving. An employed brother or sister with little free time may try to shift the load to the unemployed one. Any of these problems can renew the antagonism between siblings who forgave each other for past transgressions.

Being forced to be the sole caregiver can rip open the old injury. The chaos of a parent crisis may call the firstborn child to arms, recharging sibling rivalry. All these struggles require sensitivity as you go forward. Keeping the new comradery of your relationship will take ongoing communication and compromise.

However, the newfound bond can be mutually beneficial when an aging parent needs help. You and your sibling can research options before your mom or dad needs them. One of the greatest factors in delaying needed eldercare is sibling disagreement. If you are once again a team before a parent needs you, you can work together for the parent's best interest and avoid a possible catastrophe. Subsequent joint planning can also prevent unnecessary placement in a nursing home. Research shows that siblings who work together when parent care is demanded reduce the stress and burden on all siblings involved while increasing the quality of their parents' lives.

One of the couples we discussed earlier, Oscar and Glenda, had a group of rules for their kids. The dad, Oscar, favored the daughter, Jinx, but also made her the enforcer who kept preteen brother Fess in line and babysat new sister Snookie when the parents were working overtime. On the other hand the mom, Glenda, favored Fess, following a pattern of her own parents of always paying more attention to her own brother, Chris. Chris and Glenda patched up their differences after their mother shared past circumstances involving parental infidelity that led to Chris being the preferential sibling in their childhood.

Oscar's older sister Emily is still trying to boss Oscar around. Even though Oscar has multiple jobs and a daughter who has possible mental health issues, two siblings who are arguing all the time and a marriage that is teetering, Emily demands more from him. Their mom is showing early signs of Alzheimer's and she wants Oscar to share the care of their mother by spending a weekend a month with her so Emily can have some respite, as she is the primary caregiver.

Oscar and Glenda discuss this with the counselor they have been seeing about daughter Jinx and her cutting issues. They agree that

Oscar cannot take another weekend a month away from his jobs due to family finances. But the counselor, who works with midlife families as well, suggests some ways Oscar can help Emily and his mom from a distance.

She suggests that through the video conference on his computer, he can set up visits on a regular basis with the family. This can be done with Emily's help. Oscar, who is great with numbers, can have all of his mom's mail forwarded to him and start paying her bills online as they use the same bank, which has excellent online bill paying services. This will take this burden away from Emily. He can have little Snookie draw pictures and the two older kids write letters and send them to his mom, who can read them instantly, having a connection with Oscar's family without his going one weekend a month. The counselor also suggests a digital photo frame, which Oscar and Glenda can purchase for his mother to help her remember everybody. They can have Jinx, who is excellent at new technology, load family photos of all holidays and random pictures of the kids each week and her grandmother will have a revolving slideshow of Oscar and Glenda's family.

Oscar and his sister have a family meeting with the help of Emily's minister at church, who has been supporting her through the stress of caring for her mom. After both adult siblings hear each other's side and Oscar's proposed solutions, sister Emily agrees to try this out. She understands how Oscar is trying to help her, as he gets support for his own family issues. In order to properly meet their mom's care needs, they must realign as sister and brother and long-distance technology has helped them both love Mom best.

Sibling Challenges That Arise in Midlife

Maintaining any relationship, especially one that is tested over and over, takes a great deal of work. Reconciliation is never a smooth road and for the rest of your life you will need the skill of compromising and walking in the other person's shoes. You will also need to use your mantra to silence your "I Hate You" story when it starts to play again. This means persisting with the fitness activities you started. If you began a yoga class, continue. If counseling helped you, keep attending. Continue to exercise, journal, meditate or anything you chose to help make yourself healthy. Maintaining a renewed sibling relationship is tough work. Like a glued-together saucer, the relationship will support the cup, but ensuring that it doesn't shatter once again takes constant gentle vigilance. That union can start to give, so you have to strive not to slip back to the same old unforgiving, unhealthy state of mind.

Stepsiblings in Middle Age

Not only do many people get divorced and remarried in midlife, but aging parents do as well and we may acquire unexpected stepsiblings through a parent's unforeseen late-life marriage. The effects of these late-life unions can be a new rash of stepsiblings, introduced in your middle age. You do not have to share your bedroom with them, as stepsiblings must in childhood, but you may be forced to interact through the exploding family web. This can mean negotiating where Mom or Dad celebrate holidays and rituals with a remote, remade family.

Late-life remarriage can bring challenges to your revived brother or sister relationship through a new stepfamily. You may feel a great sense of anger and frustration if either of you disagrees about the new marriage. Some people embrace the extended families. Other siblings reject them, accepting only their blood relatives into the fold. Differing points of view can explode into a new battle.

Money matters can definitely cause a new rift. Remarriage and new stepsiblings may mean dividing a parent's estate among more heirs, resulting in a diminished inheritance. Remarried parents can leave their whole estate to a new spouse or autumnal stepsiblings. One of you may accept Mom or Dad's choice while another may boil over, prompting a new quarrel. Lawsuits can break out as the family drama escalates to the courtroom. Maintaining a united front as you face these family changes takes constant attention to shore up your reborn sibling attachment.

Modern Stepsibling Problems

Present-day parents Gayanne and Amos have been raising their step-family, composed of Gayanne's children from another marriage, Vera and Roger, and Amos's son from his first nuptials, Randy. They have had to confront sibling anger between Gayanne's daughter and son that ended in a sliced arm for Roger and an expensive trip to the local emergency room. Randy and Roger have had to share a room on weekends that was formerly all Roger's. Vera was failing in two high school classes and feeling more estranged from her peers than she already had. She is not a cheerleader type and thus was never the preppy girl who went to all the school dances with a great date.

This new remarried clan of three disparate and alienated siblings gets a great deal of assistance from extended family. Gayanne's long-divorced real parents have come to their daughter's and granddaughter's aide. Baby boomers may have topped the divorce rate amongst the generations, but they generally retain a deep commitment to their children and an abiding and sparkling love for their cherished grandchildren.

Grandmother Janet and her ex-husband Jack tackle the sibling problem in this family created by the blending of the stepgrand-children. Janet helps out daughter Gayanne by picking up grandson Roger after school and taking the boy back to her house. Making his missing baby book to make Roger feel more loved and special, she also lets him practice his drums, which have been uprooted from his bedroom when space had to be made for stepbrother Randy. Wanting to connect with her teenage granddaughter, she opens up an account on a social networking Web site and lightly comments when Vera posts something general on the social networking site. Vera engaged with her grandmother by teaching her how to get online.

Janet attempts to interact with stepgrandson Randy by being the backup driver for after-school pickup when his dad can't get him because of work.

Grandpa Jack, on the other hand, lends a real hand to stepgrandson Randy, who is a gifted student in need of a space to quietly study when he's there on weekends. Jack builds a little desk area for him in an unused alcove near the laundry room.

Janet and Jack join together to arrange a garage sale for their daughter and her family. In need of ready cash in the severe economic downturn of recent times, the family needs money and space as they jam stepbrothers Roger and Randy into one room. So the grandparents organize the garage sale, divide up duties for all of their grandkids and, at the end of the day, produce $450.00 for their daughter's family.

Over the few months, Janet and Jack have worked together to aid their daughter's family. In their efforts to end the damage that is injuring their grandkids and new stepgrandchild, their own relationship is rekindled. At the garage sale, Jack noticed Janet still has a great figure and bright white smile. She was the polar opposite of conservative Jack in the nineteen sixties, as he wanted her to stay home and be his wife while she wanted to use her college education to work. Now neither of them has to worry about that kind of demographic strain as both are retired with excellent pensions.

Jack asks Janet out to dinner and she readily agrees to go with him after they clean up the garage sale. This leads to many dates and a proposal of remarriage in about a month. Jack decides he does not have more than twenty years to live it up and he would like to do so with Janet. He says she knows everything about him, warts and all, and still has that great smile for him. Janet, on the other hand, is leery. She has tried marriage again and it did not work out. But Jack is a familiar, handsome guy who helped her through chemistry, knows her family secrets way back to her childhood and still is an emotionally and sexually fulfilling man.

Gayanne and Oscar are shocked when they hear this news. Gayanne, like many kids, has always secretly wanted her parents to get back together. Oscar thinks Jack's a great guy and he's more than happy with anything his father-in-law wants to do. The grandchildren are mystified. Vera feels embarrassed at even the idea of her grandparents having sex, which she assumes is going on. Roger is a little young to think much about it, but Randy is incredibly happy. Jack and Janet have really been there for him to give him a hand in blending into this new family. So Gayanne, Oscar and their three blended siblings are all in attendance for Jack and Janet's second wedding at the county court house.

Tammy and Paula's Conflicts over Caregiving

Paula and Tammy are two sisters who met and resolved their childhood break. Revealing her "I Hate You" story, Paula reconciled with her youngest sister. She created a mantra to banish the "Tammy is the favorite" refrain if it started playing in her head. Her new mantra is "I will be kind to myself and be my own favorite."

The bridal party in Tammy's gala wedding finally included Paula's little girl. Through the ongoing support of her good friend Pat, Paula continued to pursue self-help activities. She enrolled in a forgiveness class at the local wellness center and worked at being in the moment, not morphing back to the second-best kid. She has also maintained her ongoing connection with all her other siblings.

But a crisis cropped up in the family that overrode all the dikes Paula and Tammy had built to bolster their new connection.

Their father decided that he and their mom should move to a smaller house by a golf course, near where Tammy lived. As Tammy was a real estate agent, she helped her parents locate the property. It seemed to meet all their social, fiscal and physical needs. A few friends from Dad's Rotary Club and Mom's bridge club already lived there, so the relocation seemed perfect. Feeling that this move endangered her whole past safe space, Paula was secretly against the relocation. In spite of this, she volunteered to help with the move. However, her parents rejected her aid, saying Tammy had already arranged for a professional mover. Her dad suggested that she tend to her own kids instead. Paula began to feel slighted again, but tried to hold her jealously at bay. The professional mover divided up the items the parents could not fit in their new home. Paula told her parents that she wanted the rocker her mother nursed the children in as babies. The moving professional took care of it, Paula was told. One day Paula went over to Tammy's house and discovered the rocker in Tammy's bedroom. Even though Tammy and Paula had stitched up the wound, the rift once again resurfaced when Tammy seemed to become her parents' favorite.

"I will be kind to myself and make myself my own favorite," had been Paula's mantra after she and Tammy reconciled. But this parental crisis seemed to wash those words right out of her vocabulary and that old drama line came blaring back in. Each time her aging mom or dad said Tammy's name, Paula's mind screamed, "Tammy is the favorite!" Tormented by jealousy once more, she was shot back into her previous train of thought.

Soon Paula reverted to her old bad habits and was getting the other siblings to gang up on Tammy. She phoned the other three and blathered on about how their mom and dad favored Tammy and neglected the rest of them. Paula sabotaged Tammy and told the other siblings that the new house was way more than their parents could afford and they had gotten a terrible deal due to the housing crash. Paula accused Tammy of only being interested in her real estate commission. As a result of this debacle, Paula screeched that all the siblings will lose their inheritances. Paula charged that Tammy didn't pay enough attention to her parents' deal as she was off planning her wedding.

After a week of angry calls, the other brothers and sisters were criticizing Tammy and all were calling her to complain. Ganging up on their baby sister, they again attacked the old favorite child. Paula felt a secret satisfaction in all the trouble she was stirring up. But, she noticed, her acid reflux also returned with the escalating drama. Recurrent stomach problems led her to see her physician, who prescribed medication, but asked if she had some new stress in her life.

Paula knew she was writhing with anger and blame again. Tammy called her one day and asked if they could all see a counselor to talk about their mom and dad's move.

Paula came to the meeting with guns blazing, telling the counselor about all of Tammy's missteps. Tammy began to sob and asked Paula why she was blaming her again. The therapist asked them both who was the parents' favorite. The old pecking order came out, and Paula put the old "I Hate You" story on the table. Once it was out in the open, Paula let go of her newfound mantra making herself the most loved and reverted to her tried and true script, blurting out that Tammy was the favorite. Her lining up the other siblings against Tammy became clear to the counselor and the sisters. The therapist helped Paula and all the siblings see how Tammy's role as the youngest had brought them all to their knees again. They all looked at their parents' downsized situation and realized the new home was the best place for them to be. Tammy explained that the professional mover mixed up the list of family items to be shared and mistakenly gave the rocker to her instead of Paula. But on the other hand, Paula had never told Tammy she wanted it, so Tammy had no clue about her desire to have it when she accepted the family treasure. They all agreed they should have had a meeting with their parents and gone through the hard part of dividing family memories themselves. Tammy apologized and gave the rocker to Paula. Meanwhile, Paula vowed to work on her mantra every day and catch herself every time she reverted to "Tammy is the favorite."

She went back to a forgiveness class she had started before her "I Hate You" story surfaced. She talked about the recurring accusation running through her head like a car spinning its wheels on an ice patch. The therapist suggested forgiving that thought, gently telling it to go away and kindly repeating "I will care for myself and make myself the favorite" every time she heard it. He told her it took years of practice, and she would be challenged over and over to be kinder to herself.

Tammy and Paula patched up their second breach and re-spliced their family tie. Paula had to adjust her own thoughts and replay that mantra with higher volume every time she heard the old mantra "Tammy is the favorite" blaring in her mind.

Daryl and Mike's New Friendship

Let's look back at brothers Daryl and Mike. The roots of their conflict started early in childhood when they were set up to be rivals. Their parents launched them into lifelong competition. The battle ranged from which baby took the first step to who had the pricier house, car and pool. Mike usually won, while Daryl despaired that he would never be the favorite son.

Daryl penned his "I Hate You" story after months of weight training and aerobics, established in his own healthy lifestyle.

Ready to talk, he and Mike met at a quiet bar near their parents' house. Daryl shared his sense of inadequacy spurred by their differential treatment.

Mike pointed to his own thick belly and laughed, slapping Daryl on the back. "We're big guys now, we can let this go," chuckled Mike. Patting his midriff, "Maybe you can help me lose these love handles." Daryl felt his old sense of second-best begin to lift and gave his brother a high five. He invited Mike to go to his weight training class to work on his paunch and abs. Understanding Mike's personality traits had changed in middle age, he saw the generous guy who his brother is today. But Daryl realized he had worked hard to get himself to this moment. It took consciously adopting a healthy lifestyle and sharing his age-old feeling of second best to move him to finally share his feelings with his older brother. Daryl's own commitment to treat himself more tenderly got him to the meeting in the neighborhood bar. Mike had been ready to resolve their intense competition for years, but Daryl had to see improvements in his own emotional and physical strength before realizing he no longer had to slug it out with his brother.

We need to see that we ourselves are that message. We must dig our hands deep in our past and find that "I Hate You" story. After unearthing your history you can transform your present by being your own fairy godmother. You create your ball gown and carriage out of the past by telling your "I Hate You" story. Moving to the moment is the magic wand that allows you to reinvent yourself. Forgiveness lets you realign your own stars.

As a midlife sibling, you can morph from the angry wild thing of your past to an adult who can happily share the midlife banquet with your brother or sister. You can shape your own internal debate each time blaming breaks out by telling yourself you are already a winner, because of your own kindness.

❧ Conclusion ❧

Twenty Tips for Raising Young Siblings

Let's look at the steps that young parents need to take to raise happy siblings today. Raising and parenting siblings is part craft. It is also part intuition and information wired into our brains. Nature wants our progeny to survive, so bitter things happen to fledglings, much like that first eaglet pushing its rivals out of the nest so it can survive on the limited food at hand. The biggest embryonic shark that eats its siblings in its mother's womb is just another case of the Darwinian principal that the strongest of the species is meant to survive. However, these early sibling deaths portray the hard knocks a species takes to genetically move forward.

What a species cannot predict is its environment—the circumstances in which our human species grows up. Circumstances, as we have covered, can be environmental disasters like a tsunami, drought or plague and they can also be social and financial tempests. You have The Great Depression of the nineteen thirties, an economic catastrophe that caused many parents to raise their siblings with an extreme loyalty to each other, prompted by desperate fiscal times. This is also somewhat mirrored in the first decade of the twenty-first century, when there was a similar economic collapse tearing apart the nests of young parents. The difference is twenty-first century families do not cling together like clans of the nineteen thirties. The family-centric values of the twentieth century Great Depression were wiped away by the baby boomers and the advent of divorce.

Parents today have to face the same financial privations in raising kids, but have the double whammy of extreme money woes while many raise blended families, parenting siblings who are half, step and blood all under one roof. These moms and dads can no longer default to the age-old "one for all and all for one" credo.

What are some answers for today's parents that will support them in rearing siblings? Let's go over some tips and strategies that may help moms and dads and avoid future "I Hate You" stories for their younglings.

Twenty Tips to Avoid Sibling Rivalry and an "I Hate You" Story in Teenagers and Young Children

1. Involve fathers more.
Research and experience during the Baby Boomer Generation has shown that it takes two engaged parents to resolve sibling conflict. As more women went back to work in the nineteen fifties and nineteen sixties, they began to expect dads to take a more active role in parenting. This involvement has been very slow to develop. Most Generation X moms and dads continue, like their baby boomer parents, to be both employed and trying to balance the responsibilities of work and family.

Sibling rivalry and warfare can be mitigated by not having one parent do it all; each can bring different strengths and perspectives in resolving conflict. Let us look back at Ted and John's sad sibling tale. Their mom was terribly overburdened because of her absent husband and it led to sibling rivalry that caused one brother to strike out at this sibling, causing a serious wound. The effects of this wound lasted forty years.

If you have a new baby or toddler like young parents Glenda and Oscar, sharing child care is critical to sibling mental health and harmony. Even though Oscar is especially busy working two jobs, Glenda has many responsibilities as well, balancing a full-time job with raising two kids over ten and a baby. To help their two older children adjust to Snookie, Oscar's involvement has become crucial. His active role in caring, nurturing and just having fun with these children can really make a difference in the siblings' relationships and cut down on the instances of resentment and strife between the two children.

Snookie plays two classic roles that are deadly in sibling warfare, as both the baby and the perceived favorite. These roles can create an "I Hate You" story and cause blame so thick it lasts for years. If Oscar can make more time to take son Fess to archery practice, drive daughter Jinx to her new drama group after school and take them both to ballgames in the spring, this will do much to let Jinx and Fess know that they are both loved as much as the new baby. At the same time, Glenda will have more time to nurture Snookie. They could reverse these roles and Glenda could do the driving to school activities and sports and take the older kids to plays that she loves. There need be no gender bias. If Oscar equally shares the care and nurturing of his three kids, Jinx and Fess have a greatly reduced chance of growing up with "I Hate You" stories.

2. Involve extended family.

Reach out to extended family living nearby, such as aunts, uncles, grandparents, great-grandparents or any blood or nonblood relative or friend who will help you bear the heavy load of parenting, so you can reduce present and future sibling rivalry and strife. Being able to engage the support of older family members like grandparents, who are pretty vital fifty- and sixty-year-olds in this modern age, can be a major help with this heavy lift. For instance, they can have children come to their house after school. This extended family involvement will allow you to share the burden of childrearing. If one sibling could go to his or her grandparents' after school and the other or others to another extended family member, this will go the distance for making them both feel special.

Twenty-first-century parents, Gayanne and Amos, are trying to make a second marriage work in spite of the increased strains on their recent marital vows. There is amplified arguing between siblings Vera and Roger and a strong sense of resentment towards stepbrother Randy.

Extended family members are your friends and can really be your midlife family rescue unit. Grandmother Janet, a baby boomer, came to the aide of her Generation X daughter Gayanne. Driving her old sedan with the peace sign on the back, she shuttles Vera and Roger to after-school activities. She also takes Roger home to her newly remodeled ranch style house, bought by her and Jack, on a regular basis, giving him one-on-one time with her. Janet is trying to make grandson Roger feel like number one when, in his own words, he felt like thirty-five when Randy moved in. Roger is able to practice his drums at Grandma Janet's, where he had to move them when they took up too many square feet in his own bedroom, after his mom jammed stepbrother Randy into half his space.

Janet made tentative overtures to stepgrandson Randy. She knew that she had to take it slowly, because Randy already had two other grandmothers and Janet was just the third wheel at this point. But Janet offered to pick Randy up after school when her new son-in-law Amos could not make it. He agreed and Janet came as an emergency driver with the kind of treat she knew Randy liked: her homemade chocolate devil's food cake, which he happily enjoyed while en route home. This helped her daughter and son-in-law, as they were trying to pick up and deliver three kids from school, plus made baby steps toward getting closer with Randy.

3. Get out your older child's baby book.

Siblings each need to feel special. Even if they're teenagers, sit down with each sibling and do a sort of teenage or younger child "life review." Talk about the child's histories and the narrative of that very special moment when he was first brought into the world. This shows him the strong links between his birth and your family. He was once the baby and the center of the family universe. Discuss his entrance into your life and reminisce about his first step or first tooth recorded in his baby book to trace his development in the family and how important each new way he grew was to you. Show him the very vital part he played in the family and how he fits into the "bigger picture" of your family tree.

If you do not have a baby book, use extended family or teens to help you make one. If you have just a box of old photos, spend the money to have them scanned or scan them yourself and make an online baby book. There are many products out there on the Internet that you can use to catalog your older child's baby history. If you don't have the time to do this, use extended family like grandparents to help you create this keepsake. (See http://www.babychapters.com/.) For teens, this is a way to use their hyperkinetic technological skills to tell their own stories. You can direct the sequence of the narrative, but they can be the technical and art directors, using their computer skills to create their own histories and thus learn how important they were to you when they were babies plus use their software and hardware expertise to see how they fit into the family scheme today.

4. Make a scrapbook.
If you do not have a baby book, try old-fashioned scrapbooking. You can buy a scrapbook kit at many stores. If you can't locate a local scrapbooking shop, go on the Internet and order the materials you need. You can even research how to do it online. This is a great way for baby boomer grandparents to help relieve the stressed working moms and dads and to spend one-on-one time with a child who is not getting enough individual attention. Plus this produces a missing baby book, proving that child was and is the sun in your universe.

Siblings need individual attention to tamp down strife. Scrapbooks, like baby books, can put on paper the very special people and events of their lives. These memory tomes are a chronological history told through both photos and mementos that contain pictures of family members and your child's friends, as well as souvenirs of family events like vacations, holidays and celebrations. If you have saved cards, playbills from theater productions they were in, graduation programs—anything—add those. This shows struggling siblings that there are deep connections between them and the rest of the family. It also gives them their own history book to go back to when they might be in doubt about their place in the family. Grandparents or any other elder relative can do an old-fashioned style scrapbook, using the tools of the present scrapbooking craze, even doing them in scrapbooking shops and groups, where you can create these memory binders alongside others.

Again, you could create the scrapbook online and have a teenager in the family or an extended family member with computer knowledge help you with the design and layout if you just have the memorabilia items. This is a great way to involve grandparents who have the time and the memory of their grandchildren's childhoods to draw from to create this scrapbook of childhood recollections and mark their importance. There are also two sides to this as a parent. You can not only help a child who is struggling with sibling issues and estrangement, but also gain some social outlets yourself as a parent by utilizing the scrapbooking idea. (See http://www.makeplaydough.com/scrap-booking_with_teens_best_paper_lines-28016.php.)

5. Don't make comparisons between two children.

Remember Mike and Daryl of our sibling wars? They were compared from almost day one by their parents and were always pitted against each other. The boys' mom crowed about how Mike got his first tooth before his younger brother, walked earlier and was smarter in school. All of this talk made Daryl very jealous of his brother. As they became adults, whenever Daryl saw Mike he was friendly but always felt that twinge of the green-eyed monster. Deep down inside these feelings of sibling rivalry sprung from comparisons the boys' parents made when they were little. If you want to avoid Mike and Daryl's fate for your own kids, don't pit one against the other.

6. Intervene immediately when a child hits or injures another child.

Don't allow guilt to build up or a wound to fester and create a future "I Hate You" story in your own child. Untended lesions turn into "I Hate You" stories that may have to be dealt with decades later. You, as the parent, could be a villain in that sibling tale. Avoid the future toxic narrative thread by talking to both siblings right away, offering consequences if one child injured another, but also letting the siblings know that the wound is being swabbed and bandaged by you—the parent—in the here and now. Settle the argument and heal emotional lesions by talking about what happened, not just punishing one child for harming the other. Discuss the feelings that prompted the injury in the first place to expunge the negative feelings. Perhaps change your parenting methods to rearrange sibling interaction as a result of the discussion.

Look back at Ted and John, the two boys who grew up with a single mom. You see that she was an emotionally overwhelmed and immature mother, working as a salesclerk in a local dress shop six days a week. After school Ted was cared for by John, who was psychologically confused and hurt by the impact of his dad leaving. The fun and freedom of after-school activities ended for John with babysitting. He resented the burden of Ted.

Remember how one afternoon Ted changed the television channel from John's favorite sports show. Furious, John swept broken glass in a circle outside and jammed a stool in the middle. John grabbed Ted, lifted him onto the stool and young Ted ended in the emergency room with many stitches in each foot. Their mom punished John, but since she needed him to watch Ted, she continued to leave the big brother in charge and she never talked about the incident again. Ted never forgave John and they grew up with Ted feeling like John was his enemy instead of his trusted friend, creating distance between the brothers for almost half a century.

Avoid a future "I Hate You" story like Ted's by tending to wounds right away. Injuries may seem superficial, but can be quite serious. Sibling injuries can be emotional abuse as well as physical ill treatment. But the critical step is that you talk about what happened with your children almost immediately and get each sibling's version of what occured. The significant next step is to see if you need to change your parenting behavior in any way to avoid another incident.

If Ted and John's mom had understood the long-term consequences of continuing to leave Ted with John, she could have gotten her sister Miriam to look after Ted instead of leaving him with still angry and resentful John after school. Allowing John to go back to the sports he craved and sending Ted to Aunt Miriam's would have gone a long way to putting the future "I Hate You" story in the trash and saving both siblings from half a century of estrangement.

So do not let siblings settle differences between themselves. Intervene right away and mediate the dispute quickly. Your involvement as a parent, talking to each sibling then taking that information and arbitrating the argument, is key. Save brothers and sisters the disfigurements that result from unresolved hurt feelings or actual wounds. Get to the bottom of the disagreement and see how you need to adjust your parenting techniques to a child's life, like Ted's mom, who could have avoided a future "I Hate You" story.

7. Stay positive and do parental marketing for each sibling.
If a new baby arrives, as one did for young parents Glenda and Oscar or at a more mature time as one did for Paula and Tammy's mother and father, work hard to promote self-worth to each new arrival. Encourage harmony among all the siblings, who are no longer that special "baby" and probably don't feel very favored anymore. Parents Glenda and Oscar were so consumed with caring for their baby and earning enough money to pay the bills, they had little time to make Jinx and Fess feel special. In fact Jinx felt like she was the least favorite child now after her equestrian

lessons were ended because of the tight economic times and an empty family budget. Having baby Snookie arrive then become the star of the family made Fess and Jinx feel like Neptune and Pluto compared to the shining Venus of Snookie.

Young dad Oscar helped to create a positive environment when he started to commit to doing more care of Snookie himself. His paternal involvement allowed Glenda to spend more time with Jinx, who was really careworn after she had to give up expensive equestrian lessons. Glenda went to Jinx's guidance counselor and found cheaper after-school activities. Jinx had shown an interest in working backstage at the high school theater, where her best girlfriend was in the school play. The high school counselor prompted Glenda to ask Jinx if she would like to join the theater company and Jinx said she would if she could work backstage. Glenda learned how to sew as a kid and volunteered to help the seamstress make costumes for the theater group so that she and Jinx could interact. She could do it at night after work, something she finds relaxing and as just her own private time. Glenda also asked her mom and dad, whom she feels helps her brother's kids more than her kids, to pay for equestrian lessons so Jinx could have the horse she loves back.

Tammy's family had no such rules in the parenting manual they may have followed. They did not know that Tammy would have such a negative effect on Paula and their other children as they grew up, creating a deep "I Hate You" story in Paula that resulted from losing her specialness after Tammy was born. Paula had been favored and Tammy took that away.

We cannot go back and change the past nor go forward to alter the future. But we can revise the present; young parents can learn from old resentments, encapsulated in "I Hate You" stories like the one Paula kept repeating in her head from the day Tammy was born.

So with the advent of a new baby or even a new stepchild, make sure you spread love evenly and show each sibling that he or she is special and important. This parental marketing will pay off in big dividends now and in the future by preventing an "I Hate You" story many years down the line and imperiling events in the future.

8. Encourage positive activities that siblings can do together.

Perhaps new siblings could teach another a sport like baseball, soccer or tennis. Have siblings do tasks together like helping you clean out the garage, redoing your attic as a spare bedroom or creating a holiday dinner. Have a garage sale to sell toys and belongings that your children may not need any longer, but do it together. Give jobs to everyone, like making signs and collecting cash, and have each child make money from his or her own items so there is a feeling of benefit from getting rid of items that may represent their childhood. Do not ask them to sell toys or treasures that have special meaning to them. Many times our old loved toys give us a sense of self and place. Find somewhere to store them if you have really frazzled kids or siblings.

Remember how Janet and her ex-husband Jack got together and organized a garage sale for Gayanne and Oscar, because they especially wanted to help out their grandchildren Vera and Roger and new stepgrandchild Randy. By giving the three kids a chance to work together on a project, these divorced grandparents felt like this was a win-win situation. It also gave Janet and Jack an opportunity to interact jointly, something they had not done a lot of since they got divorced forty years before. But the overarching needs of their daughter and mutual love of their grandchildren made them partners in this cause, which is really to support Gayanne in her new marriage and their grandchildren's adjustment to a stepbrother. The event was very instrumental in bettering their relationship with children and grandchildren as well as between themselves.

The chance to be a family again by each contributing to a collective task reforges the family connection and illustrates how it is never too late to bring a family together. Bonding activities that can be initiated at all stages of family life, in this case, thread the relationship, not only between grandparents and children but offer a new tie to stepchildren as well.

9. Set limits, boundaries and fair rules for kids.
Children need limits and spoken rules that are also written down so all siblings know how to behave and can repeat those set of laws out loud to each other. How siblings behave toward each other is the first social lesson they get on how to interact with the world and perhaps their future boyfriends, girlfriends, partners or spouses. It also gives siblings the framework to cooperate with each other, which will help them avoid potential battles in all stages of their life and maybe an upcoming "I Hate You" story. Give them positive rules and perimeters.

Our "I Hate You" stories show that not saying family rules aloud can be lethal to sibling relationships. Rules have to be fair and they can't be silent.

As you remember, Daryl and Mike's family rule told them to always try to beat each other at everything. The rule began with their parents pitting one against the other throughout their childhood. The family imperative was the first always wins. Midlife sibling Ginger's imperfect operating system scripted her family rule that boys get the biggest share and girls receive the leftovers. These old broken operating systems remained in Daryl's and Ginger's minds through-out their entire adulthood, substituting for the real universe in their day-to-day lives. So in order to avoid future sibling combat as a present-life parent of young siblings, set fair family rules.

Remember the difficulties Glenda, one young mother, faced with her two children fighting and at times slugging it out with one another. She was referred to a counselor through the work and family program at her job. The counselor was able to suggest many ways that Glenda could parent more successfully. One thing the therapist suggested was to set limits carefully and fairly. The counselor also suggested that Glenda say these rules out loud to her kids, plus write them down on paper or a dry erase board so they are a positive set of laws that tell everyone how to behave. Glenda started by saying baby Snookie could not have free reign to go into Fess's room and tear up his model creations. The older brother's room was now considered off limits to Snookie and this rule was written very clearly in a document that was posted on the refrigerator. Making clear rules that were fair and benefited Fess, who was acting out by slugging his older sister, in turn helped this family immensely.

The work and family counselor also suggested some positive rules for this young family. Since both older children were acting out with each other, Glenda and Oscar had a family meeting and talked about constructive ways for these kids to communicate their feelings. Instead of hitting, they encouraged the older two to use their words to tell the other sibling they were angry as an alternative to physical altercations. Glenda was also counseled to set consequences when her rules were not followed. In the nineteen seventies and eighties when she was growing up, Glenda did not have many rules, as she had warm but seemingly self-centered parents who did not offer much structure. They were loving to her, but, like some moms and dads who came of age in the late nineteen sixties, offered few boundaries for their children. Glenda believes that she became a nurse in order to counterbalance the lack of rules in her family. She sometimes feels like Michael J. Fox on the popular show *Family Ties* she watched as a kid. Like his character, young Republican Alex P. Keaton, did on the show, as a nurse she feels comfortable following doctors' orders and enjoying a structured lifestyle.

Meanwhile, her parents were like the mom and dad on *Family Ties*, a couple of aging hippies with liberal views who were married in the late nineteen sixties. And, in turn, Glenda's mom and dad were surprised their kids did not adopt the same liberal values. In fact, Glenda's brother Chris is a staunch conservative who worshiped George W. Bush, making him more like Alex Keaton than his sister in that regard. Glenda and Chris ended up setting their own boundaries as kids, but Glenda found herself parenting much like her own very liberal parents. In fact, Chris seemed to physically attack her with few consequences from their mom and dad.

Glenda, like her parents, had not forbidden the hitting that went on between Jinx and Fess. Additionally, mealtimes were pretty loose and on many occasions the family didn't all sit down together. Glenda had not given Jinx strict times to be home. The counselor suggested Glenda change all this and start implementing some fair but firm boundaries. Glenda did not have to go to extremes—too few boundaries like her parents or too many boundaries so her kids will rebel—but she should try to create a fair mix of family laws to help her kids feel safe and secure.

10. Hold family meetings.

Hold a family meeting so everyone can talk about problems before they reach crisis level—to themselves, to siblings and to the family unit. Family meetings can handle disagreements with siblings and teach them several skills. Brothers and sisters can learn the value of each other's perspectives. Siblings can learn how to negotiate and compromise through a family meeting. Siblings can individually ascertain their own worth through a family meeting and learn how to argue in a constructive way in such a setting. Parents who moderate family meetings can teach siblings how to control aggressive impulses. Parents can also teach brothers and sisters the tools they need to be in charge of themselves and offer guidelines for communicating with each other through the rules the parents set for running the family meeting.

Family rules need to be said out loud to siblings and acceptable behaviors or actions need to be negotiated. A family meeting is an excellent tool through which a parent can negotiate. Remember our chapter "Break the Rules"? The difficulty with many family rules is that they are unfair and go unstated. Examples are the gender rules that plagued Ginger and her brother Bobby, which had come down the line of many family generations.

A family meeting gives parents a chance to get rules out in the open and talk about family policy. These family get-togethers also give children an opportunity to discuss what they consider to be unfair and unstated rules and have the parents consider changing them in an open forum. Family meetings with children help establish lines of communication so rules are heard and siblings have less reason to fight, hurt each other or suffer long-term sibling wounds over rules that were never spoken, such as the ones about favored genders from prior generations.

These meetings allow siblings to solve problems as a team. This is a great skill for brothers and sisters to gain early, because when they reach midlife, they may have to come back together, like Ginger and her brother Bobby and make plans for how to care for an aging parent or help Mom move or aid another sibling or even a relative. If siblings gain the skills for solving problems fairly in a group and among themselves, they will go a long way in gaining a model to use when they are older. Family meetings give all siblings a forum to be heard and have their opinions respected. This helps to boost each child's self-esteem.

Family meetings give a parent opportunities to delegate responsibility or fairly reassign responsibility if it is divided in a way that one child is more burdened than another. An example of this is Jinx, who feels unfairly burdened by taking care of Snookie, while brother Fess changes few diapers. We can fast-forward to the midlife problems of Ginger and Bobby. Ginger handles all the caring for her mom, while Bobby, the dentist, does little to assist his sister. This sets up a huge schism between the two that actually started in their childhood, as it has in the lives of Fess and Jinx. The family meeting suggested by Glenda's counselor could go a long way to more fairly divide caregiving tasks early in her children's lives.

Parents should initiate the family meeting and be the moderators so there are boundaries and they can ensure that everyone's voice is heard. It is important as a parental mediator that the parent be impartial throughout the family meeting. If differences come up, allow the siblings to work it out through the "Go Around" exchanges with you, the mom or dad, enforcing the rules of listening and allowing everyone to have his or her say. It is important that arguments in the family meeting do not get out of control, so the mom or dad needs to moderate in a way that expressions of feelings are allowed but within control so the dialogue can take place and actual solutions can be reached. The family as a team can decide when and where to hold the meetings. Family meetings are more effective with young families if they are short, around fifteen minutes.

Parents can remind family members to communicate in a supportive way and help siblings hone critical listening skills. Refer back to chapter 8 if you need tips on listening skills. These same listening skills apply to families of all ages and are critical tools in family meetings. Getting everyone to contribute can be achieved with kids in a format called "Go Around." A parent can start with a topic, like what happened this week that made you feel good, then go around the circle and ask each child to contribute. You can then go around to something that bothered you. Siblings can use a "Go Around" to verbalize what another sibling did to make them mad or upset. Parents who are the moderators need to acknowledge feelings that are articulated. Ask open-ended questions to clarify the difficulty and encourage everyone to contribute ideas for solutions.

Let's look back at Glenda and Oscar's children. The work and family counselor from Glenda's job suggested that she and Oscar hold a family meeting with their children. There were issues centered around baby Snookie that were causing Glenda's two oldest children to act out and were actually impacting her own ability to work.

When Glenda held the family meeting with Oscar and her two kids, Jinx and Fess were able to talk about what they felt was an unfair rule. The rule was they had to babysit fourteen-month-old Snookie after school when the day care center dropped her off back home on the days Glenda had to stay late at work. The siblings ended up squabbling between themselves about who changed Snookie's dirty diapers and who babysat her. Both kids also felt it was unfair that they had to watch Snookie while their homework and activities didn't count.

This family meeting gave each person in the family a chance to describe his or her feelings and be heard.

You can create a family meeting agenda and e-mail it to all the older kids who have computers and can read your report aloud to younger kids. Parents can take minutes or have a child take minutes by hand or on their laptops, then have that child e-mail the minutes to all the family members. Minutes should include the decisions or new rules that the family made during the meeting. This is a fun way both to have kids participate and to use the technology they love. You can also post both the agenda and the minutes on the refrigerator or any place where all family members can see them.

The goal of a family meeting is for everyone to have the opportunity to speak, including children, set mutual goals for the family and help implement changes in the family rules and routines. Family meetings don't have to be used just for problems but can be used for positive things a family will do, such as planning a trip or a vacation or a garage sale where all the kids will make money from their older items or donate money to the church or a social cause the family may collectively choose. They are meant to build and support the family as a whole but also establish ethics in each individual child.

Meetings with children give parents a chance to air rules that may be unstated and get them out in the open. An example is a gender rule that says more is expected of daughters as far as caring for younger kids than of sons, like the gender disparity with Jinx and Fess over changing Snookie's diapers. The family meeting can be used to get out in the open such problematic rules as comparisons between siblings that rarely are talked about but can create sibling wars for decades, as in the story of midlife siblings Mike and Daryl.

The habit of family meetings will help your sons and daughters have a forum to work together the rest of their lives. As parents need care and assistance as they age, family meetings are one of the best tools for siblings to rally around each other and delegate tasks while they decide what to do. If you as a parent create this habit when they are kids, you are not only teaching them how the family settles disputes, but also how they can plan and delegate such issues in the future. It serves as an insurance policy for you in your future.

11. Create a team spirit.

Children and siblings need to learn how to act as a team. As they grow up, their team will have to be reconstituted many times—for rituals, for rites of passage and to take care of aging parents. Teach them how to act as a team now when they are young in order to learn social relationships among themselves at an early age. Look at who will be the leader and the followers. Is there a fair leader? Does she or he treat the followers fairly?

Team spirit among siblings is a critical tool. Remember the generational team spirit created by the Depression era cohorts. Because of the crushing economic woes of the nineteen thirties, siblings grew up tutored in team spirit and loyalty to each other by their parents. This spirit continued as they reached retirement and continued to age. Their parents' emphasis on "one for all and all for one" lasted a lifetime. Creating a team spirit is just as important now among siblings. Working together teaches siblings to share, to delegate responsibility and to really appreciate each other. This cuts down on sibling rivalry and squabbles and builds a deep bond that the siblings have for a lifetime.

Remember siblings Angie and Jennifer: Their parents in their second marriage had no idea that they should act together to teach stepsisters Angie and Jennifer how to be a new blended family. All Angie and Jennifer gained out of their parents' new marriage was estrangement, which took many decades to undo.

Tammy and Paula and, to a lesser degree, all the siblings in their family suffered. Because Tammy was deemed the favorite and her parents did little to nurture the self-worth of all the older children after she was born, Tammy and especially Paula were estranged. When it came time for Tammy's wedding, Paula had no model for team spirit and didn't want her daughter to be Tammy's flower girl. Neither Tammy nor Paula was ever taught team spirit by their parents, sentencing them to years of sibling misery.

Gayanne and Amos's new blended family was certainly in need of team spirit. With new stepbrothers Randy and Roger sleeping in a carved-up room and Roger and Vera skirmishing so much that Roger was injured, this group needed a way to act as a cohesive unit with a team strength. Grandmother Janet and grandfather Jack banded together again after decades of divorce to help this family achieve family cohesiveness. By putting together the family garage sale, giving each child a role, allowing the kids to reap the financial rewards from some of their own items, planning the sale together and letting Gayanne and Amos have a role, Janet and Jack evoked team spirit. Just as they displayed team spirit in spite of their own divorce, they hoped these warring siblings, who were banded together not by choice but by remarriage, would learn a way to work together as a unit.

12. Promote empathy.
Teach siblings how their behavior affects other siblings in order to avoid catastrophes in the future.

Remember siblings Angie and Jennifer? Angie felt like a modern day Cinderella and she saw stepsister Jennifer as Drusilla, her evil stepsister. Angie finally decided to write her "I Hate You" story, because she suffered through so many years of psychic pain. She and Jennifer met and Angie was surprised that Jennifer had her own tale of woe about her parents' divorcing and growing up in a stepfamily. Angie was able to see the other side of her stepfamily stories and what Jennifer had gone through as a child, something she had no idea about when they were young. So Angie finally was able to have empathy for Jennifer, an emotion that helped her forgive her sister and bring them back to an aligned sibling relationship.

Parenting your children so that they are sensitive to each other's point of view is important for exposing sibling issues and diffusing blame and hurt that can turn into sibling wounds, then scars, then sibling "I Hate You" stories. Family meetings, spending one-on-one time with each child and emphasizing that child's self-worth can give each sibling a forum and a reason to be sympathetic and empathetic to the others and avoid sibling wars now and in the future.

In their adult years, Ted finally gained compassion for his brother John after decades of having no empathy for his older brother. When Ted, at last, told his "I Hate You" story, after learning bits of the bigger picture in his family, his brother apologized. Empathy was still not gained. After a several-month forgiveness layaway plan, Ted finally trusted his brother enough to really have empathy for what caused sibling John to hurt Ted in the first place. If you teach your children empathy now, you can help them avoid years of estrangement and battles and true strides toward brotherly love can be achieved early.

Here's how empathy can be taught by parents: Use some basic psychological tools. Allow a child to describe his or her own feelings. Help two arguing siblings to explain to you how each one is feeling, not what the other brother or sister made them feel. This matches "I" words with feelings. "I feel angry or happy or sad" — not "the way my brother took the toys away from me made me feel mad." We are modeling empathy as parents by assisting siblings in putting their extreme reactions and feelings into words.

- **Model empathy.** When a child makes a mistake like breaking a plate, provide emotional sustenance as parents by not blaming but offering understanding that accidents can happen. Treat pets kindly and with affection to teach how kindness counts in all people's and animals' lives.

- **Assist siblings in learning to read facial expressions and interpret body language.** When children are young and you as a parent read books to your kids, point to the facial expressions and signal emotion like kindness or anger. Reinforce kindness and explain how our actions sometimes bring on anger and how we can understand it and dispel it in others like siblings.

- **Talk about how people's actions can elicit feelings in others.** Perhaps a schema like "Your brother looked so happy when you let him play with your fireman set. Did you notice his large smile?"

- **Practice empathy at home.** "The cat is meowing and brushing on your leg. Do you think you could give him several pets?" "Your sister is having a hard time opening that jar and her face looks unhappy. Do you think you might help her unscrew it?" "Grandpa is having a hard time getting those birthday boxes out to his car. Could you carry some out for him? That would be so kind of you."

13. Teach siblings to be fair gender-wise.

Treat your own children fairly gender-wise and do not favor one sex over the other. This will teach them they are both equal.

Let's look back to Ginger and Bobby's sibling trouble and Ginger's "I Hate You" story. Her family favored Bobby over Ginger because he was the son. This was something that many generations of parents before Bobby and Ginger had rules about. Their parents learned this gender bias from their parents before them.

However, let's look back at what Ginger was able to do when she created a new intention to change the rule in her own family as a mom. She and her husband committed to treating their three children equally. After taking care of herself by journaling and other health activities to improve her self-esteem, Ginger told her "I Hate You" story to her brother and changed the way she parented her own daughters and son gender-wise.

Then Ginger inventoried her judgments with her two daughters and son and decided to dust out the murky corners of her own sexual bias. She rubbed out her parents' rule that only girls do housework and now Ginger's son and daughters do the same number of chores after school. Her older daughter excelled in biology and Ginger and her husband paid for her to attend a local university science camp set up to encourage girls to choose a career in that field. Her younger daughter was a whiz in school woodshop. Ginger's husband owned a construction company, so rather than box their daughter in a stereotypic female role, Ginger and her husband felt clear-eyed about their daughter's entrance into what was historically considered to be a boy's world. Finally all her kids were encouraged to go to college and Ginger and her husband promoted higher education for all. Ginger has moved from the negative past to a positive present by focusing equally on her daughters and son. She altered her family pattern so that her children would not repeat the past then recycle it to yet a newer generation, creating a never-ending dysfunctional loop. She has done all this in spite of her brother Bobby not accepting her feelings in her "I Hate You" story.

When young mother and father Glenda and Oscar found out their daughter Jinx was showing signs of cutting, it triggered a cascade of realizations about their children's problems. Glenda went to the Human Resources department at her job right away and started counseling through her work and family program. She discovered one of the many problems leading to Jinx's cutting was a gender bias both she and her husband had inherited from their own parents. Oscar's family favored girls, but made them the enforcers and expected them to do all the work. Glenda's parents had favored her brother. With new baby Snookie, both parents had expected teenager Jinx to take a large load of child care plus do her own schoolwork. They had to stop her horseback lessons because of the financial meltdown of the family and the American economy. Fess had not been tasked with many diaper changes and had not lost any extracurricular activities. Through counseling they realized they had to change their gender bias toward their children.

14. Give children a chance to work things out themselves.

If there are small issues, like an argument over a toy or who gets a cell phone, tell siblings the consequences of not settling the argument—no one gets the phone, you both will have to set the table every night or no one plays with the toy. Walk away and give them a chance to settle the issue. With big issues, like one child hurting another, parents need to intervene right away and solve the problem—heal the wound immediately before it becomes a scar. If you do not, the children will become a victim and a victimizer and create "I Hate You" stores of their own.

Glenda and Oscar had a family meeting to discuss the bigger issues in their family, like how the teenagers were asked to babysit little Snookie when the parents were not home from work. Under the guidance of the counselor, the parents arranged another form of day care. But Jinx and Fess still will be home alone at times, because Oscar has two jobs and Glenda sometime stays overtime at the hospital when other nurses, midwives or doctors are late for shifts. She does not refuse the added hours, because the family needs the extra money in these hard economic times.

Glenda and Oscar arranged after school activities for the siblings, but there will always be times when the kids will have to settle arguments themselves. This means that Fess and Jinx will have to figure out how to end disputes between themselves without their parents' intervention. Many steps are taken to this need for the warring siblings.

Jinx is going to one-on-one counseling for her cutting issue and that counselor helps her discuss some ways she can avoid arguments with her brother in the future. The parents in the family meeting introduce the idea that everyone communicates better using "I" words. This communication technique plus listening skills that the parents discuss in family meetings have cut down on the hitting and punching that Jinx and Fess had been doing when they are home alone.

Young parents Gayanne and Amos have a situation where their children Roger and Vera got into a fight so heated a window pane shattered in the door when the glass cut Roger's arm and he was rushed to the hospital where he received several stitches. Gayanne and Amos could not let their children work this out themselves. They sought out counseling for both kids at that point.

Gayanne and Amos decided to have a family meeting at the suggestion of their counselor and encourage Randy, Roger and Vera to verbalize their everyday frustrations. Beyond listening as parents, Gayanne and Amos started to teach all their kids new ways to communicate with one another. In their recently blended family there has been very little open communication among the three stepsiblings. The parents realized they must tutor them about how to interact, because they will be siblings now for life; that is, if this marriage lasts. The parents' future as a couple may depend upon the blended brothers and sister learning how to talk to one another and settle differences when Mom and Dad are not present.

Angie and Jennifer didn't learn to communicate for decades until Angie told her "I Hate You" story. Angie has learned the value of using "I" words in preparing to tell her "I Hate You" story. She scripted her story in "I" words. Listening skills were another communication technique that Angie learned through the process of preparing her "I Hate You" story for Jennifer. Angie and Jennifer's mom and dad, who remarried in the nineteen sixties, had no clue about teaching their stepchildren how to communicate. They really had no idea that Angie and Jennifer would have a problem learning how to be a family. When it was evident that there were troubles, neither Angie's dad nor Jennifer's mom stepped up to the plate to get some help for the wounds that were being gouged.

So to prevent the "I Hate You" stories that might be in your young children's future, start now to teach them good communication skills so they can fairly settle issues among themselves. If big issues like hitting or emotional wounds occur, treat the wounds right so that you don't have one child ending up feeling like a victim, as Angie did, and one child looked on as the victimizer, as Angie viewed stepsister Jennifer.

It is important that clear communication skills are taught to your young children, whether blood siblings, half siblings or stepsiblings.

15. Make every child your favorite.
Parents need to be impartial in every way, although this is a very difficult skill to learn. It is inevitable that moms and dads will feel differently about offspring who have varying needs, dispositions and places in the family. However, treating each child as equally important will stop an "I Hate You" story from ravaging sibling relationships. Parents have to practice being fair and impartial to each of their kids every day, even though it can be difficult.

Find a reason to tell each child he or she is special and spread the love equally. Having favorites creates giant "I Hate You" stories. If you praise one child, make a conscious effort to praise the others.

In the new family created by Amos and Gayanne, Roger, Gayanne's former youngest, was no longer the baby of the family as new stepbrother Randy was actually younger than he was. Randy was the only child of Amos and his former wife. Although he was the apple of his mother's eye, he was the second act in this new family, as he was living in his stepmother's house and she had two of her own children. One of these blood children, Roger, had to share half his bedroom with Randy, which set up potential bad blood between the new siblings. So both stepbrothers had each lost their favored status and were wounded by their demotions.

Dual-role dad Amos began to remedy the sense of favoritism in his household after he and Gayanne went to counseling. He started to spend one-on-one time with his son at Randy's new home, Gayanne's original residence before she married Amos. Randy was doing a science project to build a trebuchet in school. He was studying the Medieval period of European history and a trebuchet is a siege engine that was used in the Middle Ages either to smash masonry walls or to throw projectiles over them. Randy sort of felt he was laying siege to his dad's new family and emotionally demolishing their house.

He and Amos went shopping for all the parts and tools they needed for the trebuchet, including a new drill and a chop saw Randy required to help build the project. Randy and his dad started to assemble the parts and put together the required science project in Amos and Gayanne's garage each weekend when his dad had him as part of the divorce settlement. This made Randy feel a little more like he was the favorite in his dad's world and also gave him a greater feeling of ownership of his alien new home.

In Gayanne and Amos's present-day family, son Roger felt like his starring role had been taken away through his mother's remarriage. He is no longer the only son, since his mom now has a stepson in Randy. He is no longer the baby since Randy is a little younger. On top of that he no longer even has a whole room to himself. Grandmother Janet, the baby boomer, came to the rescue in her old sedan with the faded bumper stickers on the rear window, one saying "Warning: Opinionated Feminist." This made Roger want to have her pick him up a block away from school, but he loves his grandma, so he gets in the car when she picks him up at the curb.

By taking Roger a few days a week, Grandma Janet is really contributing to solving these sibling difficulties. Roger feels like the favorite again each time she puts him in her old car, with the magic wand of his grandmother's one-on-one attention. She makes a baby book for him, which her daughter never had the time to do.

Janet knew that Roger felt his mom was not paying the kind of interested attention she used to lavish on her only son. So Janet pitched in to show Roger that he was a favorite of hers. She changed her own schedule, which had included going to the gym three afternoons a week and volunteering at the local women's shelter. She started a major project, a historical dig with him to show her grandson he had once been the center of the family and a much-photographed and loved little baby. Janet was sort of doing recent genealogy, given that eleven years had passed since Roger's birth and she had to make sure each picture in Gayanne's box was really of Roger and not of Vera. Gayanne did not label each photo, being overwhelmed by a new baby and toddler at the time.

Janet's efforts gave Roger a sense of family history and how he fit in as the very special last born. Her excavations into the family past also bonded her more deeply with her daughter Gayanne, as Janet's divorce had scarred their relationship.

16. Listen to both sides.

Help children to grow up without lasting emotional or physical scars. Attend to wounds right away and be there to referee squabbles between siblings, because they will come up all the time. Show a respect for each point of view; listen to both sides. Schedule a block of time with your kids to do this if you work long hours. Have children engaged in after-school activities so they don't come home and argue in an unsupervised environment.

Again, family meetings are an excellent tool for letting you listen to both sides of a sibling argument. They provide a safe arena where you can impose rules with each person taking a turn to express his or her viewpoint regarding it. Parents can also set rules in the beginning about no interrupting, so each child can say what he or she has to say without another one butting in. At the family meeting you can ask each sibling to share his or her concerns and use the "Go Around" technique as mentioned earlier, where each person at the meeting gets a chance to respond to the topic. So if the "Go Around" topic was "what happened this week that you didn't like" and one sibling said something the other sibling did made him mad, this method would give the other siblings a chance to respond in a safe and democratic environment. You are listening to both sides of the issue.

Keep in mind the stories of Ted and John and how their mother sought a doctor's care for Ted's physical injury on his feet, but never tended to his emotional wound of being really afraid his big brother would harm him again. As we've seen, this ended up as a decades-old "I Hate You" story with Ted being unsure of himself and still seeing himself as a victim in midlife with John in the role as the perennial culprit. It took Ted writing down his "I Hate You" story, then tending to his own emotional wound by seeking counseling himself in his forties to repair the relationship between him and his brother John. If their mom had sought counseling or another form of outside help to listen to both sides, this would have gone a long way to avoid this "I Hate You" story and its subsequent emotional scars.

On the other hand, young parents Gayanne and Amos responded to an incident in which their kids got into such a pushing match on either side of a glass-paned door that it resulted in Roger with a bloody gash and a trip to the emergency room, similar to Ted's childhood dilemma. But this serious situation between her two children prompted Gayanne to take her kids and the entire family to counseling. Tending to the wound right away set the stage for a positive outcome, so there would be no festering emotional injury, no "I Hate You" story and no lifetime of blame between her two kids.

17. Maintain family rituals and introduce innovative new ones.
As we have seen in our previous chapters, rituals are the glue of family life. They patch up disputes and give us a forum for a year full of celebrations to mark family history. They are the touchstones for rites and family passages and keep us gathering over and over again to celebrate and observe those landmarks. Rituals also give form to our daily routines and are the counterpoints of the turning clock when the family can gather and talk, share and gossip. Breakfast, lunch, tea, dinner and bedtime are all ritual occasions for families to gather. So to avoid sibling squabbles with younger family members, start with the day-to-day passages. Try to schedule regular meals where everyone is invited to sit down and share. Even if it is occasional fast-food meal, frozen dinner or take-out order, these daily gatherings can bring siblings and new members of the family together.

Gathering for ritual occasions like anniversaries, holidays and family reunions allow you to spend special occasions together as a family. This quality time experienced together gives kids and their siblings the tools to solve problems, negotiate, compromise and learn the skills of working together as a team.

Celebrate passages like each member's birthday, including those of the older generation. If you are too busy as a parent, have grandparents or extended family who may have more time bake the birthday cake, hold the party at their home or go to a restaurant. You can create new rituals for a blended family or a family that has new siblings whether they be half, blood or step.

At the counselor's suggestion, Gayanne and Amos made Halloween a big celebration for their family to try to better include Randy in the sibling mix and give Vera and Roger new ways to bond with stepbrother Randy. Gayanne and Amos put on costumes, and after the kids had trick or treated; they let everyone dive into their candy while the parents lit candles and turned out the lights. Everyone then told ghost stories. Grandma Janet and Grandpa Jack also donned costumes and came to the event. The witch's garb and fake bloody vampires' masks gave everyone the anonymity to talk, allowing the siblings to interact in a less direct but more fun way. The ritual was so well received it was repeated each Halloween and got more fun each year. In essence, the family had expanded this holiday ritual with ceremonies of their own that were exclusively special to this family. Gayanne and Amos' blended brood created their own holiday ritual they could repeat for years to come. In doing that they included new sibling Randy and helped him form a deeper bond with Vera and Roger. The ritual also defined them as a new family. Perhaps their children, when grown up will create similar occasions.

18. Spot siblings who are acting as victims and victimizers.

Remember red flag number three in the beginning of the book? If a child believes he or she is the victim and a sibling is the scoundrel, there is a serious sibling problem. If one child feels like the helpless person and the other sibling has all the power, this may lead in years to come to an "I Hate You" story.

As we have seen in previous chapters, feeling like a victim can turn into a lifelong pattern. Remember Ted and John again from earlier chapters. Ted perceived his brother as the scoundrel all his life, never understanding the circumstances around why John had gotten so angry that it led to his injuring Ted. Even though John never hurt Ted like that again, Ted grew up with an "I Hate You" story as their mother never got to the bottom of why big brother John was frustrated enough to do something that hurtful. Ted became the perennial victim in all parts of his life. He had to enter counseling in midlife to learn how to speak up for himself. Ted joined a variety of social groups to tug himself out of the victim role.

Give siblings the tools to use different ways to communicate anger and frustration, like words. Don't rush into therapy, but deal with less serious issues yourself to step up to the plate as parents so you will keep hitting that ball for your daughters and sons.

19. Raise caring brothers and sisters.
Harmony is more than a sound. It is difficult to slug it out, bully or emotionally batter a person about whom you really care. Caring for your brothers and sisters and being kind to them is the first lesson we give our children on how to be kind to the world. One major role as a mom or dad is facilitating harmony among children. You cannot and should not make them act in accord, but create the conditions that result in a comfortable relationship among them. You can't have power over every action taken by each sibling, but you can shape their relationships. Without burdening him or her, allow the oldest child to do things for the youngest. Have one child teach another how to do something. Give each one separate tasks, which contribute to the family and work together for a common goal.

20. Spot blaming behavior.
Listen for negative comments about one sibling by another that get repeated over and over and may lead to a future "I Hate You" story. Remember red flag number one for "I Hate You" stories was these

repeated experiences. Jinx blamed baby Snookie for ruining her social life, because she couldn't be on her cell phone or online when she had to babysit her little sister. Through the work and family program at her job, mom Glenda and dad Oscar were able to spot this blaming story and fix circumstances leading to Jinx having to babysit. They paid for emergency day care for Snookie to get Jinx out of babysitting. They also worked to get Jinx involved in the after-school drama group so she had supervised socialization. Many good outcomes were envisioned for this daughter by these parental changes. One outcome was that Jinx would not grow up with an "I Hate You" story about Snookie, the new special baby, the way that sibling Paula kept telling the story of "special Tammy" thirty-five years later. As a parent you want to intercede when you hear this kind of sibling blame.

Stepsibling Roger told his mom, his teacher, his grandmother and his grandfather all the same story, over and over. The tale was how he had to give up half of his room to Randy. Although a heart-breaking story in itself, it is a red flag for a future "I Hate You" story. His mother Gayanne, Grandmother Janet and new stepdad Amos heard the alarm bells of the repeated story and although they could not build a new bedroom right away, they did many things to make Roger feel special and not broken in half as he perceived his room.

Recall what we noted in the beginning chapters of the book. Siblings are the longest relationship of your whole life. They are with you in the nursery and are still there in your old age. They are a longer relationship than those with your spouse or your own children as they are always in the same timeframe as you. As parents, we have an exhausting job description that includes being referee, psychologist, drill sergeant, coach, teacher and nurse. One of the most important roles we can have is as a teacher to our children about their lifelong bond. They not only need to understand that this bond will persevere til death, but also need to know how to keep that connection glued together. Unfortunately, as we have seen in this book, negative childhood experiences may rip at the fabric of siblings' relationships and make them break away from each other. At times these tears turn into "I Hate You" stories. But as we have learned, siblings can reconnect. However, it is far better to never break apart in the first place.

Look back at the "I Love You" stories in this book and teach your young children how, as siblings, to have a team spirit, how to gather in a family meeting when they need to discuss critical family topics, how to observe family rituals together and the many other ways they can create their own "I Love You" stories with siblings. By giving your children these tools, they will learn strategies to avoid new "I Hate You" stories and find out how to forgive past sibling transgressions in order to create a healthy, happy future together.

❧ **Acknowledgments** ❧

For all their support, careful reading, patience and contributions to the text, we would like to acknowledge Penny Warner, Connie Pike, Julia Gallo, Anne Beggs, John A. De Rugeris, Ken De Rugeris (who was crucial in the drive to finally get this book published), Karen Zellin, Eiko Ceremony, Pat Ihrig, Kaila De Angello, Athan Bezaitis, Martha Alderson and Marsha Keefer. Thanks to all of you for your kind gifts.

❧ Notes ❦